LITERATURE REVIEW JUNE 2012

Teaching Adolescents To Become Learners

The Role of Noncognitive Factors in Shaping School Performance: A Critical Literature Review

Camille A. Farrington, Melissa Roderick, Elaine Allensworth, Jenny Nagaoka, Tasha Seneca Keyes, David W. Johnson, and Nicole O. Beechum

TABLE OF CONTENTS

ACKNOWLEDGEMENTS We would like to recognize the many people who contributed to this review. Our research colleagues at the University of Chicago Consortium on Chicago School Research and our practitioner colleagues at the Network for College Success gave critical feedback and helped us think through the implications of the existing literature for both research and practice. We would particularly like to thank Eliza Moeller, Faye Kroshinksy, Kersti Azar, Kafi Moragne, Thomas Kelley-Kemple, Mary Ann Pitcher, Sarah Howard, Rito Martinez, Jackie Lemon, Catherine Whitfield, LaKisha Pittman, Cecily Langford, Michael Kristovic, Sue Sporte, W. David Stevens, Marisa de la Torre, Julia Gwynne, Bronwyn McDaniel, and Penny Bender Sebring for their feedback on our model of noncognitive factors and their critical comments on and contributions to the report. We are indebted to members of the CCSR Steering Committee who provided substantive feedback on our research, particularly Lila Leff and Kim Zalent. Angela Duckworth and David Yeager gave us very helpful critical commentary that strengthened our final product. CCSR Associate Director, Communications, Emily Krone and Communications and Research Manager, Bronwyn McDaniel were instrumental in shepherding this through the production process. Welcome to baby Caroline Mary Phillips, whose conception and birth coincided very closely with the conception and delivery of this project.

This work was supported by Lumina Foundation and Raikes Foundation. We thank them for their support and close collaboration in this project.

CITE AS:

Farrington, C.A., Roderick, M., Allensworth, E., Nagaoka, J., Keyes, T.S., Johnson, D.W., & Beechum, N.O. (2012). *Teaching adolescents to become learners. The role of noncognitive factors in shaping school performance: A critical literature review.* Chicago: University of Chicago Consortium on Chicago School Research.

This report was produced by UChicago CCSR's publications and communications staff: Emily Krone, Associate Director, Communications; Bronwyn McDaniel, Communications and Research Manager; and Jessica Puller, Communications Specialist.

Graphic Design by Jeff Hall Design
Editing by Ann Lindner

The University of Chicago Consortium on Chicago School Research created this report in partnership with **Lumina Foundation** and **Raikes Foundation**. We gratefully acknowledge their substantive intellectual contributions and financial support.

RAIKES FOUNDATION

Raikes Foundation provides opportunities and support during adolescence to help young people become healthy, contributing adults with a special interest in improving outcomes for early adolescents (ages 10 to 14). As early adolescents transition into middle school, they enter a challenging developmental period, the stakes for academic performance are higher, and their choices can have lifelong impact. This is also a critical stage for identity development; young people establish beliefs about their capabilities and potential, develop patterns of behavior around learning, and cultivate the relationships with peers and adults that impact their sense of belonging. Raikes Foundation's early adolescent grantmaking aims to develop each young person's agency by building the mindsets and learning strategies that support youth in productively persisting through middle grades and on to college, career, and life success. Raikes Foundation primarily invests in the development of programs and practices, inside and outside the classroom, to intentionally build critical mindsets and learning strategies among low-income early adolescents. Raikes Foundation also supports research and efforts to raise awareness of the importance of mindsets and learning strategies to youth success.

LUMINA FOUNDATION

Lumina Foundation is committed to enrolling and graduating more students from college. It is the nation's largest foundation dedicated exclusively to increasing students' access to and success in postsecondary education. Lumina's mission is defined by Goal 2025—to increase the percentage of Americans who hold high-quality degrees and credentials to 60 percent by 2025. Lumina pursues this goal in three ways: by identifying and supporting effective practice, by encouraging effective public policy, and by using communications and convening capacity to build public will for change. Lumina has worked with and made grants to many colleges, universities, peer foundations, associations, and other organizations that work to improve student access and outcomes across the nation.

THE UNIVERSITY OF CHICAGO CONSORTIUM ON CHICAGO SCHOOL RESEARCH

The University of Chicago Consortium on Chicago School Research (CCSR) conducts research of high technical quality that can inform and assess policy and practice in the Chicago Public Schools. CCSR seeks to expand communication among researchers, policymakers, and practitioners as it supports the search for solutions to the problems of school reform. CCSR encourages the use of research in policy action and improvement of practice, but does not argue for particular policies or programs. Rather, CCSR researchers help to build capacity for school reform by identifying what matters for student success and school improvement, creating critical indicators to chart progress, and conducting theory-driven evaluation to identify how programs and policies are working. A number of features distinguish CCSR from more typical research organizations: a comprehensive data archive, a focus on one place—Chicago, engagement with a diverse group of stakeholders, a wide range of methods and multiple investigators, and a commitment to sharing research findings with diverse publics.

BACKGROUND OF THIS REPORT

Early in 2011, Program Officers from Lumina Foundation and Raikes Foundation approached researchers at CCSR about undertaking a joint project, focused on the role of noncognitive skills in students' school performance and educational attainment. In addition to their financial support, Lumina and Raikes brought their respective interests and expertise in postsecondary attainment and middle grades education. CCSR brought its trademark approach to school reform: using research and data to identify what matters for student success and school improvement, creating theory-driven frameworks for organizing the research evidence, and asking critical questions about the applicability of research to practice.

Noncognitive Factors

School performance is a complex phenomenon, shaped by a wide variety of factors intrinsic to students and in their external environment. In addition to content knowledge and academic skills, students must develop sets of behaviors, skills, attitudes, and strategies that are crucial to academic performance in their classes, but that may not be reflected in their scores on cognitive tests. Other researchers have described these factors as *noncognitive skills*; we broaden the term to *noncognitive factors* to go beyond a narrow reference to skills and include strategies, attitudes, and behaviors. This change in terminology suggests a more expansive understanding of noncognitive factors, requiring that we look beyond individual-level skills to consider the ways students interact with the educational context within which they are situated and the effects of these interactions on students' attitudes, motivation, and performance.

While we are strongly persuaded by the evidence of the importance of these factors for students' course performance, we find "noncognitive" to be an unfortunate word. It reinforces a false dichotomy between what comes to be perceived as weightier, more academic "cognitive" factors and what by comparison becomes perceived as a separate category of fluffier "noncognitive" or "soft" skills. As others have pointed out, contrasting cognitive and noncognitive factors can be confusing because "few aspects of human behavior are devoid of cognition" (Borghans, Duckworth, Heckman, & Weel, 2008, p. 974). In reality, these so-called cognitive and noncognitive factors continually interact in essential ways to create learning, such that changes in cognition are unlikely to happen in the absence of this interaction (Bransford, Brown, & Cocking, 2000). How could one's study skills, for example, not be part of a cognitive process? How could one's intelligence not come into play in the exercise of one's social skills? Alas, the word *noncognitive* is already deeply embedded in educational policy circles, in the economics literature, and in broader discussions of student achievement. Though we agree with others' objections to this terminology, we feel compelled to use it. To try to substitute in another word now would likely confuse rather than illuminate our collective understanding of this important area of research.

One further clarification is in order. Throughout this review, we use the term *cognitive factors* to refer generally to the "substance" of what is learned in school, namely a student's grasp of content knowledge and academic skills such as writing and problem-solving. This is distinct from a student's *capacity* to learn. Advances in cognitive science over the last 30 years have highlighted the limitations of the concept of an individual's intelligence "quotient" (IQ) as a fixed and quantifiable amount of intellectual capacity. Research in human cognition has moved away from the idea of cognition as being isolated within an individual brain to depending on the contexts in which it exists, "including the environment, perception, action, affect, and sociocultural systems" (Barsalou, 2010, p. 325). Barsalou summarizes 30 years of research in cognitive science by saying that "continuing to study cognition as an independent isolated module is on the fast track to obsolescence." In our review, then, we work from the idea that learning is an interplay between cognitive and noncognitive factors and that intelligence is embedded in both the environment and in socio-cultural processes.

CHAPTER 1

The Promise of Noncognitive Factors

Over the past 20 years, changes in the U.S. economy have raised the stakes for educational attainment, resulting in dire economic consequences for workers without a high school diploma and some college education. American adolescents have responded by dramatically increasing their educational aspirations; almost all high school students in the U.S. now say they expect to go to college (Engel, 2007). Education policymakers have attempted to ensure students' qualifications for college by ratcheting up academic demands through more rigorous high school graduation requirements, increasing participation in advanced coursework, and raising standards within courses. Test-based accountability measures have been enacted with the intention of holding schools accountable for reaching these higher standards.

Currently, there is considerable optimism around the new Common Core State Standards, with expectations that this articulated framework of content knowledge and core academic skills will lead to more high school graduates who are ready for college and the workforce. There is also growing consensus that schools need to "ramp up" expectations in the middle grades, resulting in policies to start the study of algebra in eighth grade, for example. Many states and districts are simultaneously developing measures of high school and college readiness that rely on specific patterns of coursework (e.g., AP courses) and standardized test scores as readiness benchmarks. These efforts suggest that students' readiness for high school or college depends almost entirely on their mastery of content knowledge and academic skills as developed through the courses they take.

Unfortunately, there is little to no rigorous evidence that efforts to increase standards and require higher-level coursework—*in and of themselves*—are likely to lead many more students to complete high school and attain college degrees. Current policy efforts rest on the assumption that a more rigorous high school curriculum will improve student performance on standardized tests, which will reflect that students are better prepared for college. But what matters most for college graduation is not which courses students take, or what their test scores are, but how well students perform in those courses, as measured by their high school course grades.[1] Students' course grades, grade point average (GPA), or class rank are vastly better predictors of high school and college performance and graduation, as well as a host of longer-term life outcomes, than their standardized test scores or the coursework students take in school (Allensworth & Easton, 2005, 2007; Camara & Echternacht, 2000; Geiser & Santelices, 2007; Hauser & Palloni, 2011; Hoffman, 2002; Hoffman & Lowitzki, 2005; Moffat, 1993; Munro, 1981; Tross et al., 2000; Zheng et al., 2002). GPA is not only important in predicting whether a student will complete high school or college; it is also the primary driver of differences by race/ethnicity and gender in educational attainment (Allensworth & Easton, 2007; Jacob, 2002; Roderick, Nagaoka, & Allensworth, 2006). **Box 1.1 and the Appendix (p. 102)** further illustrate this point.

The findings on the critical importance of GPA for students' future outcomes suggest that we need to better understand why they are so predictive of later success. Grades must capture some other important student attributes—over and above the content that test scores measure—but what? The prevailing interpretation is that, in addition to measuring students' content knowledge and core academic skills, grades also reflect the degree to which students have demonstrated a range of academic behaviors, attitudes, and strategies that are critical for success in school and in later life, including study skills, attendance, work habits, time management, help-seeking behaviors, metacognitive strategies, and social and academic problem-solving skills that allow students to successfully manage new environments and meet new academic and social demands (Conley, 2007; Farkas, 2003; Paris & Winograd, 1990) (**see Figure 1.1**). To this list of critical success factors, others have added students' attitudes about learning, their beliefs about their own intelligence, their self-control and persistence, and the quality of their relationships with peers and adults (Ames & Archer, 1988; Bandura, 1997; Bandura & Schunk, 1981; Keith, Keith, Troutman, Bickley, Trivette, & Singh, 1993; Pintrich, 2000; Schunk & Hanson, 1985; Wentzel, 1991; Zimmerman, 1990). There is a long list of factors—beyond content knowledge and academic skills—shown to have an impact on student performance.

Economists refer to these factors as "noncognitive" because they are not measured by commonly administered cognitive tests such as IQ tests or academic examinations. In a wide range of studies, many of these noncognitive attributes are shown to have a direct positive relationship to students' concurrent

FIGURE 1.1

Factors Measured by Test Scores versus Grades

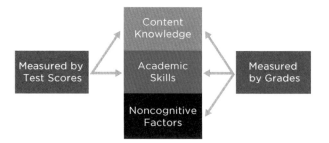

school performance as well as future academic outcomes. Economist and Nobel laureate James Heckman (2008) argues that noncognitive factors such as motivation, time management, and self-regulation are critical

BOX 1.1

Measuring Academic Performance: The Case for Focusing on Grades

Despite all the attention to standardized tests, a growing body of research shows that achievement test scores are not strong predictors of whether students will graduate from high school or college. Research on early indicators of high school performance finds that passing courses and GPA in the middle grades and even earlier in elementary school are among the strongest predictors of high school outcomes (Kurlaender, Reardon, & Jackson, 2008; Neild & Balfanz, 2001; Zau & Betts, 2008). Likewise, high school grades are stronger and more consistent predictors of college persistence and graduation than college entrance examination scores or high school coursetaking (Geiser & Santelices, 2007; Roderick, Nagaoka, & Allensworth, 2006). In a study using data from the University of California, Geiser and Santelices (2007) found that high school grades were a stronger predictor of both college GPA and likelihood of college graduation than students' SAT scores, class rank, and family background.[2]

In *Crossing the Finish Line*, Bowen, Chingos, & McPherson (2009) also found that high school grades were much better predictors of college graduation than ACT or SAT scores. Like others with similar findings, Bowen and colleagues speculate that, beyond measuring content mastery, grades "reveal qualities of motivation and perseverance—as well as the presence of good study habits and time management skills" and "often reflect the ability to accept criticism and benefit from it and the capacity to take a reasonably good piece of one's work and reject it as not good enough" (p. 124). Ultimately it is these qualities, more so than content knowledge, that signal which students are likely to excel in their studies and persevere in their schooling.

Furthermore, it is not just course grades and educational attainment that are better predicted by grades than by tested performance. Miller (1998) found that high school grades had strong, significant relationships with earnings nine years after high school, for both men and women, even after controlling for educational attainment and school effects. Earnings were higher by about 20 percent for each GPA point earned in high school (As versus Bs; Bs versus Cs; Cs versus Ds). Hauser and Palloni (2011) found that students' class rank (as determined by their grades) accounted for all of the relationship between IQ and length of life, and suggested this was due to having established responsible patterns of behavior during adolescence.

These findings make sense. Students who come to class and complete their work are likely to have developed the kind of work habits they will need in college as well as in the workforce. Students who struggle with self-discipline or productivity in high school will likely find the challenges of college overwhelming, regardless of their intellectual ability or content knowledge. The finding that course grades matter over and above achievement test scores suggests that grades do indeed capture something important about students that test scores do not.

for later life outcomes, including success in the labor market. Recent research on noncognitive factors has not only suggested their importance for student academic performance but has also been used to argue that social investments in the development of these noncognitive factors would yield high payoffs in improved educational outcomes as well as reduced racial/ethnic and gender disparities in school performance and educational attainment.

Interest in noncognitive factors has been propelled in recent years, in part, by some compelling results from a number of psychological studies. This body of work has shown some short-term interventions that target students' psycho-social beliefs—such as interventions that work to change students' beliefs about their intelligence, that promote social belonging, or that connect performance to future goals—as having substantial effects on school performance that are sustained over time (e.g., Blackwell et al., 2007; Good, Aronson, & Inzlicht, 2003; Oyserman, Terry, & Bybee, 2002; Walton & Cohen, 2007). Two widely cited psychologists, Duckworth and Seligman (2005), suggest that academic performance depends in large part on students' self-control or Conscientiousness, concluding that "a major reason for students falling short of their intellectual potential [is] their failure to exercise self-discipline" (p. 939). They claim that measures of self-discipline are far more predictive of positive academic outcomes than are measures of IQ. Carol Dweck and her colleagues (2011) conclude in a review of the evidence on academic mindsets and what they term "academic tenacity" that "educational interventions and initiatives that target these psychological factors can have transformative effects on students' experience and achievement in school, improving core academic outcomes such as GPA and test scores months and even years later" (p. 3).

Just as importantly, researchers are increasingly turning to noncognitive factors to explain differences in school performance by race/ethnicity and gender. Brian Jacob (2002) notes that academic difficulties are often attributed to poor "noncognitive skills" among boys, including "the inability to pay attention in class, to work with others, to organize and keep track of homework or class materials and to seek help from others" (p. 590). Interventions that focus on developing academic mindsets, moreover, are being designed and evaluated as a method to reduce stereotype threat and improve the academic performance and educational attainment of racial/ethnic minority students (Aronson, Cohen, & McColskey, 2009). As we review later, much of this work shows promising results. Thus, a collection of research suggests not only that noncognitive factors contribute to students' academic performance but also that racial/ethnic and gender differences in school performance can be reduced by focusing on students' attitudes and behaviors.

Unfortunately, knowing that noncognitive factors matter is not the same as knowing how to develop them in students. And what exactly is the nature of these noncognitive factors? Are they inherent student characteristics that some students have and others do not? Are they fixed traits, or do they change in response to context or environment? Can they be taught and learned in a school setting? Are noncognitive factors more important—or more problematic—for one race/ethnicity or gender over another? Many of the big claims about noncognitive factors have little clear evidence about their implications for educational practice. The suggestion that educators would see big returns from developing academic mindsets, self-discipline, and other noncognitive factors rests on the assumption that these factors are malleable and that educators or researchers have practical knowledge of how to change them. It also requires that educators understand the potential payoffs of different approaches to developing student noncognitive factors, that they have concrete strategies to address their development, and that tools exist to reliably measure changes in these factors.

If indeed noncognitive factors are malleable and are critical to academic performance, a key task for educators becomes the intentional development of these skills, traits, strategies, and attitudes in conjunction with the development of content knowledge and academic skills. In essence, teachers would play a vital role in helping students move from being passive recipients of academic content to active learners who can manage their workload, assess their progress and status, persist in difficult tasks, and develop a reliable set of strategies to master increasingly complex academic content as they proceed through school.

5

While evidence increasingly suggests that college and career readiness is driven by more than just content knowledge and core academic skills—that noncognitive factors play a key role in student success—it is unclear how all the different types of noncognitive factors interact to shape academic performance or what their implications are for educational practice. Studies of noncognitive factors often examine one particular skill, mindset, or behavior in isolation, making it unclear how all of these factors work together to affect student outcomes. There is, as yet, little coherence to the broad array of research findings and claims around the role of noncognitive factors in students' performance in school. In this report, we seek to bring this much-needed coherence as we review the research on noncognitive factors with a focus on students in the middle grades, in high school, and in the transition to college. We are particularly interested in identifying which noncognitive factors matter for students' long-term success, clarifying why and how these factors matter, determining if these factors are malleable and responsive to context, determining if they play a role in persistent racial/ethnic or gender gaps in academic achievement, and illuminating how educators might best support the development of important noncognitive factors within their schools and classrooms. In reviewing the literature, we use students' course grades as the outcome of interest. For each noncognitive factor, then, we examine the research evidence on the relationship between that factor and students' course grades or GPA, which we refer to broadly in this report as "academic performance."

In Chapter 2, we bring together the existing literature into a conceptual framework that organizes the broad body of research on noncognitive factors. In this framework, we identify five general categories of noncognitive factors related to academic performance: 1) academic behaviors, 2) academic perseverance, 3) academic mindsets, 4) learning strategies, and 5) social skills. We evaluate the research evidence behind each of the five categories in Chapters 3 through 7 in order to identify gaps in the knowledge base and help policymakers and practitioners judge potential high-leverage points for improving student achievement. For each category, we review the research evidence, asking:

- How is this factor related to academic performance?
- Is this factor malleable?
- What is the role of classroom context in shaping this factor?
- Are there clear, actionable strategies for classroom practice?
- Would changing this factor significantly narrow existing gaps in achievement by gender or race/ethnicity?

Table 9.1 on page 78 summarizes our review of evidence on noncognitive factors, organized by these five questions.

After reviewing the evidence on the five noncognitive categories, in Chapter 8 we examine the implications of this work for student learning at three key points in an adolescent's educational trajectory: the middle grades, entrance to high school, and the transition to college. We present case studies on these three periods to shed light on the role of noncognitive factors in students' academic performance across educational transitions. The report closes with an interpretive summary and recommendations for practice, policy, and future research.

In this work, we try to develop a coherent and evidence-based framework for considering the role of noncognitive factors in academic performance and to identify critical gaps in the knowledge base and in the link between research and practice. We see this as a prerequisite for policymakers, practitioners, and education funders who would wish to assess the potential of noncognitive factors as levers for increasing student educational attainment. In our review, we found evidence to suggest that the best leverage points for improving student performance are in helping teachers understand the relationship between classroom context and student behaviors, providing teachers with clear strategies for creating classrooms that promote positive academic mindsets in students, and building teacher capacity to help students develop strategies that will enhance their learning and understanding of course material.

Our review shows that academic behaviors have the most immediate effect on students' course grades. In relation to behaviors, much of the recent attention to noncognitive factors focuses on the idea of developing students' "grit" or perseverance in challenging work.

6

However, despite the intuitive appeal of this idea, there is little evidence that working directly on changing students' grit or perseverance would be an effective lever for improving their academic performance. While some students are more likely to persist in tasks or exhibit self-discipline than others, *all* students are more likely to demonstrate perseverance if the school or classroom context helps them develop positive mindsets and effective learning strategies. In other words, the mechanisms through which teachers can lead students to exhibit greater perseverance and better academic behaviors in their classes are through attention to academic mindsets and development of students' metacognitive and self-regulatory skills, rather than trying to change their innate tendency to persevere. This appears to be particularly true as adolescents move from the middle grades to high school, and it again becomes important in the transition to college.

7

CHAPTER 2

Five Categories of Noncognitive Factors

Five General Categories of Noncognitive Factors Related to Academic Performance:

1. ACADEMIC BEHAVIORS
2. ACADEMIC PERSEVERANCE
3. ACADEMIC MINDSETS
4. LEARNING STRATEGIES
5. SOCIAL SKILLS

What does it take for students to graduate from high school, go to college, and persist to earn a degree? The list of potential answers to this question is long and extends far beyond content knowledge and academic skills. The noncognitive factors we considered for this review included: persistence, resilience, grit, goal-setting, help-seeking, cooperation, conscientiousness, self-efficacy, self-regulation, self-control, self-discipline, motivation, mindsets, effort, work habits, organization, homework completion, learning strategies, and study skills, among others. We pushed to clarify the meanings of a number of loosely defined concepts and to reconcile disparities between researchers from different disciplinary backgrounds (economists, psychologists, sociologists) who occasionally used different terms for similar constructs or the same terms to describe concepts that were measured quite differently. To synthesize the vast array of research literature on each of these concepts, we organized the wide range of traits, skills, behaviors, and attitudes into categories of similar constructs. We then created a conceptual framework, using empirical research and theory to hypothesize the relationships among categories and the relationship of each category to student academic performance. We describe each of the five categories briefly below, followed by a systematic review in the subsequent chapters of the quality of the research evidence in each category.

1. Academic Behaviors

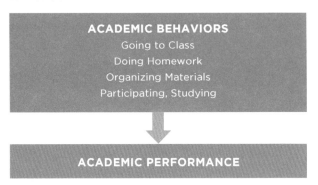

ACADEMIC BEHAVIORS
Going to Class
Doing Homework
Organizing Materials
Participating, Studying

↓

ACADEMIC PERFORMANCE

Academic Behaviors are those behaviors commonly associated with being a "good student." These include regularly attending class, arriving ready to work (with necessary supplies and materials), paying attention, participating in instructional activities and class discussions, and devoting out-of-school time to studying and completing homework. It is easy to see how these behaviors would directly relate to how well one does in a class. We start here in reviewing the relationship of noncognitive factors to academic performance because academic behaviors are most proximal to one's performance in school. Academic behaviors are the visible, outward signs that a student is engaged and putting forth effort to learn. Because they are observable behaviors, they are also relatively easy to describe, monitor, and measure. Academic behaviors are quite often an outcome of interest in evaluating interventions designed to improve students' school performance. Many programs, policies, and even curricula could reasonably be considered effective if they lead to an increase in student attendance, homework completion, studying, or class participation.

Academic behaviors are extremely important for achievement; we will show that virtually all other noncognitive factors work *through* academic behaviors to affect performance. We will return to this point in our review of academic perseverance, academic mindsets, learning strategies, and social skills, but it is hard to

8

imagine how noncognitive factors could improve student performance *without* working through the classroom behaviors that directly shape academic performance. Chapter 3 provides a summary of the research on academic behaviors.

2. Academic Perseverance

Academic Perseverance describes a set of psychological concepts with a long research history. Broadly, academic perseverance refers to a student's tendency to complete school assignments in a timely and thorough manner, to the best of one's ability, despite distractions, obstacles, or level of challenge. However, evaluating the literature on the range of concepts under our catch-all heading of "academic perseverance" proved challenging. To persevere academically requires that students stay focused on a goal despite obstacles (grit or persistence) and forego distractions or temptations to prioritize higher pursuits over lower pleasures (delayed gratification, self-discipline, self-control). Academic perseverance is the difference between doing the minimal amount of work to pass a class and putting in long hours to truly master course material and excel in one's studies. While academic perseverance is—by definition—a critical factor for students' long-term educational attainment and is often the explicit goal of the growing focus on noncognitive factors, the literature that falls under the umbrella of perseverance is not conclusive in its implications for educational practice or its generalizability to a broad range of students. Chapter 4 provides a summary of the research on academic perseverance.

3. Academic Mindsets

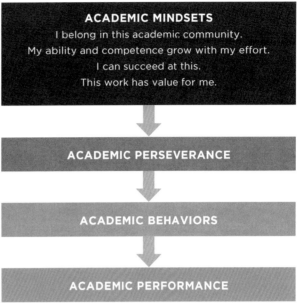

Academic Mindsets are the psycho-social attitudes or beliefs one has about oneself in relation to academic work. Positive academic mindsets motivate students to persist at schoolwork (i.e., they give rise to academic perseverance), which manifests itself through better academic behaviors, which lead to improved performance. There is also a reciprocal relationship among mindsets, perseverance, behaviors, and performance. Strong academic performance "validates" positive mindsets, increases perseverance, and reinforces strong academic behaviors. Note that this reciprocal, self-perpetuating system also works in a negative loop. Negative mindsets stifle perseverance and undermine academic behaviors, which results in poor academic performance. Poor performance in turn reinforces negative mindsets, perpetuating a self-defeating cycle.

A long history of psychological research undergirds the concept of academic mindsets. This includes foundational work in goal theory (Dweck, 1986; Dweck & Leggett, 1988); social learning theory (Bandura, 1977; Rotter, 1954); attribution theory (Weiner, 1979); expectancy-value theory (Eccles, Adler, Futterman, Goff, Kaczala, Meece, & Midgley, 1983); and the concepts of self-efficacy (Bandura, 1986) and locus of control (Rotter, 1954). Psychology research has also addressed the way context and experience can undermine positive academic mindsets, such as the theories of learned

9

helplessness (Seligman & Maier, 1967) and stereotype threat (Steele, 1997; Steele & Aronson, 1995). In Chapter 5 we review the literature on the relationship of four academic mindsets to academic performance, as well as the effects of learned helplessness and stereotype threat. Each of the four academic mindsets is briefly described here.

1. I belong in this academic community. The first mindset involves a sense that one has a rightful place in a given academic setting and can claim full membership in a classroom community. Educational theorists have long held that learning is a social activity and that understanding is constructed through interaction with others (Dewey, 1958; Vygotsky, 1978). Accordingly, students need to feel as though they belong to a community of learners and that their academic self is a "true" self (Harvey & Schroder, 1963; Oyserman, Bybee, & Terry, 2006). A long line of research evidence shows that having a sense of belonging in a school or classroom improves a student's academic performance.

2. My ability and competence grow with my effort. The second mindset rests on the belief that one's academic ability can improve in response to one's efforts, rather than being fixed at a given level and outside of one's control. Notably, across the empirical literature, one's beliefs about intelligence and attributions for academic success or failure are more strongly associated with school performance than is one's actual measured ability (i.e., test scores).

3. I can succeed at this. A third mindset that impacts the degree to which students persevere in academic work and exhibit strong academic behaviors relates to beliefs about their abilities to succeed at a given task. Individuals tend to engage in activities that they feel confident in their ability to complete and to avoid those in which they lack such confidence (Bandura, 1986).

4. This work has value for me. A fourth mindset involves a student's sense that the subject matter he or she is studying is interesting and holds value. Value can be variously defined as the importance of doing well on a task (attainment value); gaining enjoyment by doing a task (intrinsic value); or serving a useful purpose or meeting an end goal that is important by completing a task (utility value) (Eccles et al., 1983).

Overall, the evidence clearly demonstrates that the four academic mindsets outlined above each increase students' academic perseverance and improve academic behaviors, leading to better performance as measured by higher grades. When a student feels a sense of belonging in a classroom community, believes that effort will increase ability and competence, believes that success is possible and within his or her control, and sees school work as interesting or relevant to his or her life, the student is much more likely to persist at academic tasks despite setbacks and to exhibit the kinds of academic behaviors that lead to learning and school success. Conversely, when students feel as though they do not belong, are not smart enough, will not be able to succeed, or cannot find relevance in the work at hand, they are much more likely to give up and withdraw from academic work, demonstrating poor academic behaviors which result in low grades. Concepts such as stereotype threat and learned helplessness rest upon the same theoretical underpinnings and illustrate ways that positive academic mindsets can be undermined by negative contextual conditions or experiences, thus interfering with students' academic performance. Chapter 5 provides a summary of the research on academic mindsets.

4. Learning Strategies

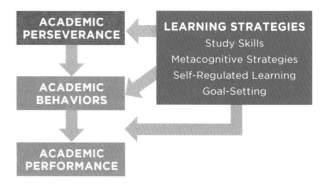

Learning Strategies are processes and tactics one employs to aid in the cognitive work of thinking, remembering, or learning. Effective learning strategies allow students to leverage academic behaviors to maximize learning. These include strategies to help one recall facts (e.g., mnemonic devices); strategies for monitoring one's own comprehension (such as while reading or doing math problems); and strategies to self-correct when one detects confusion or errors in one's thinking. Learning strategies may also include goal-setting and time management, both of which help students manage the process of learning. Unlike the research on other noncognitive factors, which comes primarily from economists, motivation researchers, or developmental and social psychologists, the research on learning strategies also draws on work in cognitive science. Helping students to learn effectively is an area of research that bridges academic behaviors (e.g., studying), subject-specific cognitive domains of learning (e.g., understanding how to divide fractions in mathematics), metacognition, and self-regulated learning processes. Chapter 6 provides a summary of the research on learning strategies.

5. Social Skills

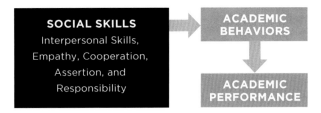

SOCIAL SKILLS
Interpersonal Skills, Empathy, Cooperation, Assertion, and Responsibility

ACADEMIC BEHAVIORS

ACADEMIC PERFORMANCE

Social Skills are a fifth group of noncognitive factors which includes such interpersonal qualities as cooperation, assertion, responsibility, and empathy. Social skills are acceptable behaviors that improve social interactions, such as those between peers or between student and teacher. Social skills repeatedly appear in the literature as important for future work and life outcomes, although their direct relationship to academic performance is more tenuous.

Development of students' social skills has long been a focus of early childhood and elementary educators. In the primary grades, educators aim to develop students' social skills to enable them to work with peers and adults to accomplish academic goals. More recently, social skills have gained increasing attention as a critical factor for adolescents in connection with career readiness. Research has suggested that employers in the twenty-first century economy need workers with "people skills" that enable them to communicate effectively, work with diverse groups, and solve problems collaboratively (Casner-Lotto, Barrington, & Wright, 2006; Murnane & Levy, 1996). While the development of social skills may be an important educational goal in itself, particularly

in the primary grades, social skills are also logically related to academic performance. For example, it stands to reason that cooperating in groups or participating appropriately in class discussions would lead to better academic performance. Perhaps social skills have a weak direct relationship with course grades because many classrooms—particularly at the high school level—still tend to rely on lecture-style instructional delivery which minimizes the social and cooperative aspects of learning. In contexts where individuals must work collaboratively in problem-solving teams, social skills are likely to be more directly related to performance.

As with our other noncognitive factors, most of the research and theory behind the development of social skills suggest that their effects on academic performance are largely indirect; they are enacted through students' behaviors in the classroom. Thus, we conceptualize social skills as affecting academic performance primarily by affecting academic behavior. Chapter 7 provides a summary of the research on social skills.

Putting Noncognitive Factors into One Framework

In reviewing the literature on these five noncognitive categories, we tried to conceptualize the relationships among factors as well as the relationship of each factor to academic performance, as measured by grades. **Figure 2.1** illustrates our working understanding of these relationships, although, as our review will make clear, much more research is needed to test the relative strengths of the paths in this model, the importance of each category controlling for the others, and the ways they interact. We anticipate that many noncognitive factors are mutually reinforcing and that relationships are often reciprocal. We used one-way arrows to illustrate the strongest hypothesized effect of each category on academic performance, but we anticipate that students' academic performance, in turn, will very likely affect their behaviors, their mindsets, their social interactions, and perhaps even their use of learning strategies. While the actual relationships among these factors are no doubt messier and more complex than indicated in the illustration, our review of the research suggests support for the ordering displayed in the model. For example, mindsets have been shown to affect academic perseverance, which

FIGURE 2.1

A Hypothesized Model of How Five Noncognitive Factors Affect Academic Performance within a Classroom/ School and Larger Socio-Cultural Context

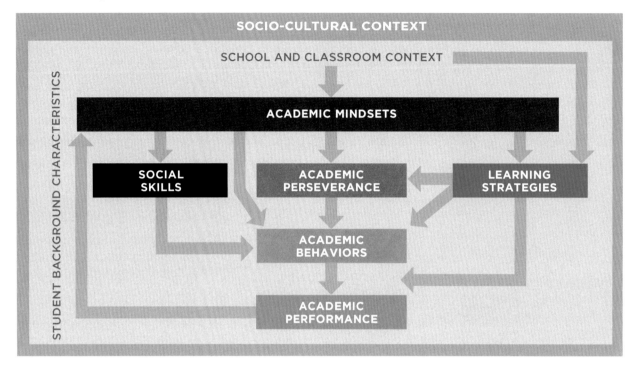

affects academic behaviors (e.g., completing work), which affects students' academic performance.

Importantly, as seen in the diagram, we set the noncognitive factors model within a "School and Classroom Context." Any given school and classroom context will reflect a wide variety of variables affecting student motivation and opportunity to learn. For example, how supports are made available and to whom, grading structures and policies, available course tracks, the ways students are assigned to those tracks, the nature of the academic tasks students are asked to do, the relationships among student peers and their orientation toward academic work, the level of safety one experiences in school, and the availability of adequate resources for learning are all important parts of any school and classroom context. Some of these variables—e.g., grading structures, feedback, and norms of behavior—are quite proximal to students' course performance and have been shown to affect academic mindsets, academic behaviors, and/or academic performance.

Note that the school and classroom context box also includes the presence of "Student Background Characteristics." For simplicity's sake, our noncognitive factors model does not specifically illustrate how these

individual characteristics are related to other factors, but we assume student background would affect virtually every aspect of the model. Student background would include all the individual characteristics a student brings to a learning situation. These include demographic variables such as race/ethnicity, age, gender, language, and socio-economic status, as well as family and neighborhood characteristics that might affect academic performance. A student's previous academic achievement (including both grades and test scores), prior knowledge, past experiences in school, and pre-existing academic mindsets are also part of his or her background characteristics. These individual academic characteristics have likely coalesced in a particular "academic identity" and degree of self-efficacy within the student, whether these are positively or negatively charged. We would anticipate that the student's previous schooling experiences and existing academic mindsets would affect his or her interpretation of any new classroom or academic work encountered. In this way, student background characteristics are very likely to mediate the relationships among the classroom context; the student's further development or enactment of noncognitive skills, behaviors, attitudes, and strategies in that classroom; and academic performance. We note too that classrooms consist of multiple individual students, creating peer effects as well as individual student effects.

Finally, we situate the model within a larger "Socio-Cultural Context" that shapes the structural mechanisms of schools and classrooms, as well as the interactions and subjective experiences of the human beings within schools. Opportunity structures in the larger society; economic conditions that shape employment opportunities as well as schooling costs; the presence of racism, sexism, and other types of discrimination that give rise to stereotypes and prejudice; and stark inequalities in resources across neighborhoods and schools all contribute to the larger context in which American students learn. The interrelationships

between cognitive, psychological, and structural variables and school performance are exceedingly complex. We offer this model as a simplified framework for conceptualizing the primary relationships among these factors, for the purpose of framing our discussion.

The next five chapters provide more detailed evidence on each of the five noncognitive factors in the model. In Chapter 8, we offer three case studies to illustrate how these noncognitive factors interact to affect students' success during specific periods of academic development: in the middle grades, the transition to high school, and the transition to college. The case studies underscore the importance of context when considering the relationship between noncognitive factors and students' academic performance.

BOX 2.1

How We Organized Our Review of the Evidence

The next five chapters review the research on each of the five categories of noncognitive factors. For each set of factors, we first want to know about its relationship to academic performance (course grades). Does the research suggest that having more of a particular factor is related to getting better grades? If multiple factors affect grades, we want to know which factors are most important because we want to know which leverage points are likely to have the biggest payoff. What are the relative effect sizes, and where are we likely to get more "bang for the buck" if we want to improve student performance? Therefore, the first and most obvious criterion for judging the state of research knowledge in a field is to evaluate the quality of the existing research and the strength of effects.

But even if a set of noncognitive factors is clearly related to academic performance, that does not mean that educators or policymakers can do anything to leverage that fact. Validating the claim that schools would get high payoffs from working on noncognitive factors requires an evaluation of whether the supporting evidence is "actionable" for practitioners. To evaluate whether the research evidence is actionable, we ask whether it is clear that the relevant noncognitive factor is malleable (i.e., do we know it can be changed), whether it is affected by classroom context (i.e., do we know that teachers can change it), and whether there are research-based strategies for developing that factor (i.e., do we know how teachers can change it through classroom practice).

A critical tension in research on noncognitive factors is the question of which factors can be intentionally developed and which are traits or dispositions that either are not malleable or are not likely to be changed by schools. Even when certain noncognitive factors are shown to be malleable and are shown to be related to academic performance, it does not necessarily follow that teachers would be able to change the factor to improve student performance. Much of the existing research on noncognitive factors is correlational (merely showing a relationship between two factors) rather than causal; this makes unclear the extent to which particular factors can be intentionally developed in classroom and school contexts, as well as whether changing them would actually improve student performance. For example, evidence that students who report high levels of self-control have higher grades than students who report lower levels of self-control does not demonstrate that the latter group of students would start earning higher grades if they were to increase their self-control. Nor does evidence of a correlation between self-control and course performance provide any guidance to teachers on how they might improve students' self-control.

It is therefore not enough for researchers to merely *identify* factors associated with better academic performance. That is a first step, but teachers and administrators also need clear research evidence about *how and why* various factors influence student performance. Then they need a set of strategies designed for use in a classroom context, aligned with their regular instructional work, to address these factors in ways that are consistent with the research. Ideally, practitioners would also have a way to track change or growth in the targeted factor to assess whether their strategies are having an effect.

Experimental studies using randomized trials, when properly designed, can yield data on both malleability and causality. For instance, researchers might show that an intervention is effective both at getting students to increase their effort and at improving their grades in class. But the *mechanism* by which these changes happen is often unclear. In much of the research we review in this report, the experiments inadvertently create a "black box" in which the actual mechanisms of change cannot be observed, leaving teachers with little understanding of why a particular intervention worked and what it implies for their practice.

For research on noncognitive factors to be action-able for practice, then, we have to go beyond merely establishing which factors contribute to students' aca-demic performance. We must also ask questions about malleability, the role of classroom context, and the availability of clear strategies that teachers can use to develop important noncognitive factors. By "classroom context," we are referring broadly to everything about a classroom that might influence student performance. This includes the teacher, curriculum, instructional practices, materials and resources, classroom policies, grading practices, behavior of peers, and all social and academic interactions that take place during a class period. All of these factors can influence whether or not students develop or choose to enact any of the five categories of noncognitive factors, in addition to affecting the development of students' content knowl-edge and academic skills.

Beyond this attention to classroom context in a broad sense, we are also interested in whether or not

there are specific classroom-based strategies that teachers can use to intentionally support students' development of noncognitive factors. For example, if a high school teacher wants to help her students develop learning strategies to use while studying geometry, what ought she to do? How can a middle school teacher best develop students' homework habits? What specifically can college instructors do to help students place a higher value on the work they do in class? It is not enough to merely know that classroom contexts have an influence on noncognitive factors. Teachers also need to understand *how* these influences work and to have specific strategies to develop students' academic behaviors, perseverance, mindsets, learning strategies, or social skills directly as part of their day-to-day work in the classroom.

Finally, we also want to examine the evidence on whether attention to any particular set of factors could make a difference in reducing educational inequality. One of the most significant claims of the research on noncognitive factors is that gaps in school performance by race/ethnicity or gender could be reduced by focusing on certain noncognitive factors. Unfortunately, researchers often ascribe observed differences in students' grades and educational attainment to gaps in underlying noncognitive factors without actually measuring these factors or establishing that there are group-based differences in these factors. By accurately measuring noncognitive factors such as homework completion or self-efficacy across race/ethnicity or gender, researchers can start to pinpoint what factors might be contributing to existing achievement gaps. In this report, we examine whether claims that certain noncognitive factors could reduce gaps in student academic performance are supported by evidence that these factors are contributing to the gaps in the first place.

To accomplish the goals described above, we structure our review of the research in each chapter to address five key questions:

1. What is the relationship of each factor to student academic performance?
2. Is the factor malleable?
3. What is the role of classroom context in shaping the factor?
4. Are there clear, actionable strategies for developing the factor as part of classroom practice?
5. Is there evidence that attention to the noncognitive factor would address racial/ethnic or gender gaps in student achievement?

CHAPTER 3

Evidence on Academic Behaviors

Academic Behaviors occupy an important place in our consideration of noncognitive factors because virtually *all* the ingredients that go into students' academic performance, whether cognitive, noncognitive, or metacognitive, are expressed *through* their academic behaviors. Academic behaviors such as completing class assignments and participating in classroom activities are how students develop and demonstrate their content knowledge and academic skills. Conversely, if a student thoroughly masters the material in a course but does not turn in homework or does not come to school to take a test, the teacher would be unable to judge what the student knows or is capable of doing. Behavior acts as a mediator of other cognitive and noncognitive factors to affect students' grades (Conrad, 2006). This is borne out by evidence as well as by theory.

What Is the Relationship Between Academic Behaviors and Academic Performance?

There is a great deal of evidence that academic behaviors play a central role In determining students' grades. For example, in one CCSR study, Allensworth and Easton (2007) looked closely at academic behaviors and their relationship to course grades and course failures for CPS ninth-graders. While students' prior test scores and background characteristics, such as gender, race/ethnicity, economic variables, school mobility, and age at entry into high school, together only explained 12 percent of the variation in ninth-grade course failures, students' absences and self-reported study habits explained an additional 61 percent of the variation in ninth-grade failures. In the Chicago study, attendance and studying not only strongly predicted course failures but also were the strongest predictors for getting high grades—more so than test scores or student background characteristics.

The single most important academic behavior may well be attending class. Attendance has a strong effect on students' academic performance, and this relationship holds true regardless of students' test scores. Moreover, small differences in attendance can have large impacts on students' grades. The lowest-achieving students entering high school in Chicago (those with eighth-grade test scores in the lowest national quartile) who had less than a week of absences per semester passed more of their ninth-grade courses than students who entered high school with test scores in the top quartile but who missed just *one more week* of class (Allensworth & Easton, 2007). The exact mechanisms whereby attendance exerts such strong effects on grades are unclear, and it may well be that different mechanisms are at work in different cases. Obviously students who are not in class do not benefit from lesson activities or instruction that they miss; this could create potential "holes" in their understanding that might impact subsequent course grades. Common teacher grading practices can also deal a strong blow to absent students' grades by disproportionately penalizing missing work. Critics have long argued for "no zero" policies to lessen the impact of late or missing assignments on students 'course grades, and several schools and districts have passed policies to that effect (e.g., Ashland SD, 2012; Dallas ISD, 2008; Pittsburgh Public Schools, 2009). Extended or repeated absences and truancy can indicate other problems interfering in an adolescent's education that would affect both attendance and course performance. But even where there are no apparent underlying issues, attendance has a stronger effect on grades and is more predictive of course failure than are students' test scores.

Beyond attending class, spending time on homework is another academic behavior shown to have a positive effect on students' grades in both middle school and high school (Cooper, 1989; Keith et al., 1993; Peng & Wright, 1994). Using a large, nationally representative sample of over 20,000 high school seniors from the High School and Beyond study, Keith (1982) conducted a path analysis and found that time spent on homework had a

15

significant positive effect on grades across achievement levels, controlling for race, background, ability, and field of study (college preparatory versus vocational). Furthermore, Keith demonstrated a compensatory effect of homework; students who scored in the bottom third on achievement tests and spent one to three hours per week on homework were able to raise their grades to Bs and Cs, equivalent to students with test scores in the middle one-third who did not do homework. If the students with test scores in the bottom third spent over 10 hours per week on homework, they could raise their grades to mostly Bs, which was equivalent to the grades of top-scoring students who did not do homework.[3] A meta-analysis (Cooper, 2006) evaluating a range of homework studies in different contexts found that virtually all demonstrated positive and significant relationships between homework and grades.

Academic behaviors can affect grades both directly and indirectly. Directly, virtually all student grades are based on student work, and completing and submitting work are academic behaviors. One might argue whether or not the content and substance of the work should (or does in practice) account for a higher proportion of a student's grade than merely the act of submitting the work, but it is important to remember that in the *absence* of submitting work and attending class, a student will fail the course. In other words, while good academic behaviors might combine with content knowledge and academic skills to earn passing grades, poor academic behaviors all by themselves can earn failing grades. Academic behaviors can also affect grades directly if teachers award points to students specifically for the acts of completing assignments, participating in activities, or even attending class.

Academic behaviors can have an indirect influence on grades as well if, as a result of engaging in the academic behaviors, students complete higher-quality work or simply learn more content and develop more skills. Students who attend class regularly and do all of their homework are likely to know more or be able to do more as a result—which would contribute to earning better grades. Indeed, across several studies, time spent on homework had a positive effect on learning as measured by both grades *and* achievement test scores (Keith, 1982; Keith & Benson, 1992; Keith & Cool, 1992;

Keith, Diamond-Hallam, & Fine, 2004; Natriello & McDill, 1986).

Academic behaviors might also affect students' grades indirectly by influencing the nature of student-teacher interactions. Teachers may have preference for students who exhibit positive academic behaviors—teachers may spend more time helping these students or more closely monitor their learning—such that students who demonstrate positive academic behaviors receive a differential instructional benefit that improves their performance in a class.

While it seems logical that attending class, studying, and completing homework will lead to better grades, there are also likely reciprocal effects—where students' success at earning high grades gives them encouragement to continue to work hard. As shown by the psychological research on mindsets, the grades students receive have a marked effect on their attitudes about school and about their own academic identities in ways that strongly influence their subsequent behavior and future school performance. While the nature of the relationships and various pathways between academic behaviors and other noncognitive factors is not yet entirely clear, the connection between academic behaviors and academic performance is strong.

Academic behaviors are so tightly bound up with each of the other noncognitive factors that they are sometimes used by researchers as proxies for these other factors. No one can directly "see" intangible characteristics such as perseverance, motivation, or a sense of belonging, but one can infer their presence or absence by the way a student behaves toward his or her schoolwork (e.g., through students' persistent effort at academic tasks, completing homework assignments, and working well with other students). Many of the studies of unobservable noncognitive factors (such as academic perseverance) are actually based on observable academic behaviors from which these unobservable factors are then inferred. For example, in a study of predictors of performance in introductory college-level courses, Kruck and Lending (2003) used students' early homework grades in the course as a measure of "student motivation or effort." Reasoning that these homework assignments are often optional, the authors concluded that "the more motivated students will do the earlier homework and quizzes and score higher grades than the less motivated students" (p. 10). Similarly, research shows that academic behaviors are largely interpreted by teachers as signs of student "effort." Where students receive a grade for effort, that grade is most often based on the teacher's observation of their academic behaviors (Brookhart, 1994, 2004; Frary, Cross, & Weber, 1993; Marzano, 2000; Nava & Loyd, 1992; Robinson & Craver, 1989; Stiggins, 1997; Stiggins, Frisbie, & Griswold, 1989).

However, the use of observable behaviors like homework completion to infer and measure unobservable noncognitive factors such as motivation or effort conflates what could be very distinct factors (feeling motivated versus doing homework), making it difficult to tease out the relationships between them or to ascertain the ways one factor might influence another to shape student academic performance. Conflating observable and unobservable factors creates the possibility of misdiagnosing poor academic behaviors in any given instance (erroneously attributing them to a lack of perseverance, for example) and makes it difficult to pinpoint the leverage points whereby teachers, parents, or others might intervene to help improve student performance.

Are Academic Behaviors Malleable?

Human behavior generally is viewed as malleable. While it may be difficult to change one's personality or one's core values, a basic tenet of psychology is that it is almost always possible to change one's behavior (Deci & Ryan, 1985; Skinner, 1953; Staats, 1963). Virtually all educational reform efforts rest on this basic assumption. Whether through new policies, programs, structures, supports, curricular materials, or instructional approaches, the premise underlying all efforts to improve schools is that students, teachers, and school leaders can be motivated, mandated, cajoled, or trained to act differently in the classroom. Students' academic behaviors *can* change. The important question is *how* educators can best facilitate these changes in ways that promote student learning and course performance.

What Is the Role of Classroom Context in Shaping Academic Behaviors?

The evidence is quite clear that classroom context shapes students' academic behavior. If we keep in mind that academic behaviors are the medium through which all other cognitive and noncognitive factors are expressed, then it stands to reason that any ways in which classrooms affect any of those cognitive or non-cognitive factors could also shape academic behavior. For example, classrooms may affect students' mindsets by creating excitement about an upcoming project. If that excitement translates to more active engagement in and completion of the project, then the classroom context will have affected behavior by working through mindsets. Likewise, if classroom instructional practice helps students develop learning strategies that allow them to derive more tangible benefits from the time they spend studying, they may be more likely to study. If teachers present material in a way that makes it more accessible and students feel like they understand what is going on, students are more likely to engage in classroom discussions. Thus, classroom context shapes academic behavior indirectly through other non-cognitive factors, as well as affecting behavior directly through behavioral expectations and strategies.

Are There Clear, Actionable Strategies for Developing Academic Behaviors as Part of Classroom Practice?

There have always existed a wide range of classroom-based and school-wide strategies for improving students' academic behaviors (e.g., increasing attendance, reducing tardiness, bringing materials to class, completing homework, promoting active participation in discussion). These mostly fall into the category of "local practice wisdom," and surprisingly few of these have been empirically studied on a large scale. For example, teachers use a range of strategies to support students in completing homework, such as: providing clear and explicit directions and expectations for assignments; requiring students to write assignments into planners (that schools often provide for this purpose); starting homework assignments in class to "get kids going"

17

and to troubleshoot any problems before students get home; and setting up procedures for students to collect missed work when they are absent. Unfortunately, few of these individual teacher-selected strategies have been rigorously or systematically studied or evaluated.

Still, we do have evidence of the effectiveness of some classroom strategies focused on academic behaviors. Research suggests that academic behaviors such as course attendance and assignment completion can be affected by the degree to which students' performance is closely monitored, with teachers or other adult advocates intervening when students' behavior falls below expectations. CCSR's work in Chicago shows that course attendance and grades are better in schools where teachers provide close monitoring and support for students (Allensworth & Easton, 2007; Allensworth, Sebastian, Gwynne, & Pareja, 2012; Stevens et al., forthcoming).

Several programs external to the classroom that emphasize monitoring and support also have been shown to have positive effects on students' grades and retention in school. For example, programs in which teachers or other adult advocates monitor students' attendance and grades to provide support when students start having problems have been shown to significantly improve students' academic behaviors and performance. Potentially effective school-wide initiatives include student advisories (Galassi, Gulledge, & Cox, 1997; Van Ryzin, 2010) and programs such as Check & Connect and ALAS (Larson & Rumberger, 1995; Sinclair, Christenson, Evelo, & Hurley, 1998). Whole school reform approaches such as the Talent Development High School Model—which houses freshmen in a Ninth Grade Success Academy emphasizing closer student-teacher relationships and additional supports—have also been shown to improve students' academic behaviors as measured by attendance rates, course passing rates, and promotion rates to the next grade level (Kemple, Herlihy, & Smith, 2005).

In short, while teachers and schools utilize a wide range of home-grown strategies to improve students' academic behaviors, few such individual strategies have been formally evaluated by outside researchers on any large-scale basis. Some whole school reform models show effects on students' academic behaviors, but it is unclear which aspects of these comprehensive models were most responsible for changing student behavior. Moreover, short of adopting these models entirely or knowing which aspects of the model to replicate, the whole school reform research provides little clear direction to teachers, other than to emphasize the importance of ongoing monitoring and support—two elements which are also supported by other studies as important to students' academic behaviors.

Would Changing Academic Behaviors Significantly Narrow Achievement Gaps?

While some researchers have claimed that differences in academic behaviors contribute to achievement gaps among different racial and gender groups (e.g., Duckworth & Seligman, 2006; Jacob, 2002), these differences only account for a limited portion of existing gaps. In Chicago, CCSR researchers looked at the extent to which students' attendance and study habits contributed to differences in students' grades by race/ethnicity and gender (Allensworth & Easton, 2007). The gender gap in GPA decreased by 21 percent after taking into account students' course attendance and study habits, and differences in failure rates decreased by one-third. Attendance and study habits explained none of the racial gap in grades, when comparing students with similar test scores and economic status. In fact, the racial gap increased once students' study habits were taken into account. African American students received lower grades than White students with similar test scores, attendance, and study habits.

In his analysis of data from over 10,000 students from the National Educational Longitudinal Study (NELS) which followed a nationally representative sample of eighth-graders from 1988 to 1994, Jacob (2002) found a slight gender difference in academic behaviors in eighth grade, when boys reported doing 5.87 hours of homework per week compared to girls who spent 6.21 hours per week on homework (0.34 hours per week difference). That gender difference in behavior decreased to 0.11 hours per week by twelfth grade, with boys and girls reporting weekly homework time of 9.74 hours and 9.85 hours respectively. Jacob did not report homework data by race/ethnicity.

Overall, there is evidence that academic behaviors explain part, but not all, of the gender gap in grades. There is little evidence that academic behaviors explain differences in grades by race/ethnicity, particularly when controlling for test scores and economic status.

Summary of Research on Academic Behaviors

ACADEMIC BEHAVIORS
Going to Class
Doing Homework
Organizing Materials
Participating, Studying

↓

ACADEMIC PERFORMANCE

Academic Behaviors are the most proximal noncognitive factors to student academic performance. Virtually all other factors that affect school performance—including content knowledge, academic skills, student background characteristics, and the full range of noncognitive factors—exercise their effect through students' academic behaviors. This suggests that there are multiple indirect pathways to improving academic behaviors (by targeting these other factors) in addition to those strategies that directly target behaviors. There is strong evidence that academic behaviors are a major determinant of course grades and that improving students' academic behaviors would increase students' course performance. There is also strong evidence that academic behaviors are malleable and affected by classroom context, and there are some clear strategies for classroom practice around monitoring and support. However, there is little evidence that working solely on students' academic behaviors would eliminate gaps in course grades by race/ethnicity or gender. Furthermore, given the pivotal role of academic behaviors in academic performance, the number of rigorous studies testing the effects of specific strategies to directly improve students' behaviors is surprisingly small.

CHAPTER 4

Evidence on Academic Perseverance

In Chapter 3, we made the case that academic behaviors are the noncognitive factor that most immediately affects a student's course performance. But high performers in school do not simply *do* the things necessary for good grades, they do them *well*. Academic perseverance is a concept that, in its most basic form, addresses student effort and the resulting *quality* of academic behavior. By quality we refer to the intensity, direction, and duration of a student's academic behavior. An academically perseverant student would behave in an engaged, focused, and persistent manner in pursuit of academic goals, despite obstacles, setbacks, and distractions.

Academic Perseverance requires not only an initial surge of momentum in a focused direction but also the ability to maintain that momentum regardless of what gets in the way. As a result, students with academic perseverance would continue working hard for a good grade in a challenging class even after failing several tests, and they would continue looking for new ways to understand difficult material instead of giving up. Academically perseverant students also would be more likely to achieve longer-term academic goals, such as earning consistently high grades over time, graduating from high school with a good GPA, qualifying for and getting admitted to a desired university, or completing a college degree. In essence, academic perseverance represents a desirable quality of academic behavior that seems essential for both short-term and long-term educational achievement and degree attainment.

The concept of "academic tenacity" has gained recognition in recent years as an important factor underlying students' academic performance. As it has been defined, however, this term incorporates a range of noncognitive factors that are conceptually quite distinct. In a working paper commissioned by the Gates Foundation, one of the most widely cited manuscripts on the topic, academic tenacity is defined as the "mindsets and skills that allow students to look beyond short-term concerns to longer-term or higher-order goals, and to withstand challenges and setbacks to persevere toward these goals" (Dweck, Walton, & Cohen, 2011, p. 5). This definition not only encompasses whether students work hard or see work through to completion despite obstacles but also incorporates the factors that affect perseverance—the mindsets and skills that underlie student persistence. Specifically, according to this expanded definition, whether or not students display tenacity can be affected by their academic mindsets (which encourage or inhibit continuing effort), their academic skills (which make it easier or harder to complete tasks), whether they have learning strategies (which make their efforts more effective), and their innate personality. While there is strong evidence that these factors are associated with academic perseverance, there are reasons for keeping them conceptually distinct from the degree to which one persists in academic work. As educators think about how to improve students' academic performance, they need to understand the specific mechanisms through which they can affect change in the degree to which students persist at tasks. Thus, we ultimately found it most helpful to separate out the demonstration of perseverance from the factors—such as mindsets—that influence it.

Even when we distill academic perseverance to center on the idea of persistent effort in school, the psychological literature identifies various kinds of persistence, each with potentially different implications for improving students' academic performance. In this review, we focus on two related concepts: "grit"—the degree to which students stay focused on a long-term goal despite obstacles; and self-control—whether students forego short-term temptations to prioritize higher pursuits (related to delayed gratification and self-discipline).

Grit and Self-Control

The idea of "grit," from University of Pennsylvania researcher Angela Duckworth, is one conception of perseverance that has gained much attention in the popular press. *The New York Times Magazine* recently ran a cover story on the importance of "character" to school and career success which prominently featured Duckworth's research (Tough, 2011). Another conception of perseverance is captured by the concept of self-discipline or self-control, and the related idea of delayed gratification. As we asked our five framing questions of the research on grit and on self-control, we found that these two sets of literature sometimes produced very different answers, with potentially different implications for classroom practice. In reviewing this work, we rely heavily on the work of Duckworth and her colleagues; she has been the most prolific researcher developing and studying these concepts over the last several years, and it is her work that is generally cited in this area.

Grit is how world-class performers and high achievers—whether musicians, athletes, doctors, actors, inventors, or business leaders—get to the top of their game. In a TED talk in 2009, Duckworth emphasized that it takes at least 10 years of sustained practice to truly become an expert in any given field (Duckworth, 2009). Grit is what allows a select group of people to sustain that effort. Duckworth, Peterson, Matthews, and Kelly (2007) refer to grit as "perseverance and passion for long-term goals" (p. 1087). They emphasize this *long-term* quality, noting that "gritty" individuals will work steadfastly on one significant goal over a prolonged period. Grit, they argue,

> ...entails working strenuously towards challenges
> [and] maintaining effort and interest over years
> despite failure, adversity, and plateaus in progress.
> The gritty individual approaches achievement
> as a marathon; his or her advantage is stamina.
> Whereas disappointment or boredom signals to
> others that it is time to change trajectory and
> cut losses, the gritty individual stays the course.
> (pp. 1087-1088)

Duckworth and colleagues developed the Grit Scale, a 12-item self-report questionnaire, to measure what they saw as the two distinct dimensions of grit—consistency of interests and persistence of effort. Importantly, the Grit Scale was designed to identify a trait that was not specific to or dependent upon any given context but rather that would characterize an individual's general tendency to persist in pursuit of important long-term goals over several years duration. Gritty individuals are those who strongly endorse statements like "I am a hard worker," "Setbacks don't discourage me," and "I have achieved a goal that took years of work," and who dismiss as "not like me" statements such as "My interests change from year to year," "I become interested in new pursuits every few months," and "I often set a goal but later choose to pursue a different one" (Duckworth, Peterson, Matthews, & Kelly, 2007). Based on studies that link students' responses on the Grit Scale to later educational outcomes, Duckworth et al. conclude that grit "is essential to high achievement," over and above the contributions of intelligence and ability (p. 1088).

Duckworth and her colleagues draw a distinction between grit and self-control, conceptualizing self-control as the ability to avoid impulsive behavior and fulfill *short-term* obligations (Duckworth, Peterson, Matthews, & Kelly, 2007). Tied to self-control is the ability to delay gratification, because part of self-control involves resisting temptations to veer from one's course and being able to put off treats or rewards until one meets a goal or finishes a task. Self-control is largely a matter of making choices of one thing over another in the short term. Duckworth and Seligman (2006) give examples of how students might exhibit self-control in school-related situations by engaging in behaviors such as "reading test instructions before proceeding to the questions, paying attention to a teacher rather than daydreaming...choosing homework over TV, and persisting on long-term assignments despite boredom and frustration" (p. 199). The researchers reason that grit and self-control—as measures of long-term and short-term goal pursuits, respectively—could well have differential effects on academic performance. Where course grades require an ongoing series of small exercises of self-control (to overcome "hourly temptations"), educational attainment (e.g., a college degree) may well be more dependent on long-term persistence over years.

In multiple studies, Duckworth and colleagues sought to identify noncognitive factors that distinguished the very top performers among other high-achieving peers in a variety of contexts: West Point military academy, the Scripps National Spelling Bee, the University of Pennsylvania undergraduate psychology department, and a private preparatory school. The researchers were interested in two related questions: In elite settings, what besides intelligence or talent sets apart certain "exceptional individuals" who distinguish themselves as the best of the best? And what accounts for the difference between highly intelligent people who are high achievers and highly intelligent people who are not? The researchers wanted to understand if either grit or self-control helped to explain extraordinary achievement. Unfortunately, because these studies are focused on understanding variables that affect outstanding achievement among groups of high achievers, their findings cannot easily be generalized to broader populations. Still, their findings of relationships between grades and grit or self-control suggest that academic perseverance—however defined—does contribute to academic performance among students with strong academic skills.

What Is the Relationship Between Academic Perseverance and Academic Performance?

A number of studies have examined the relationship between academic perseverance—whether defined as grit or self-control—and educational outcomes. Two pertinent studies examined the relationship between college students' grades and their grittiness as measured on Duckworth's Grit Scale. In a relatively small sample of undergraduates at the University of Pennsylvania ($n = 139$), when controlling for SAT scores, grit was associated with college GPAs ($r = 0.34$), roughly equivalent to the association between GPA and SAT scores ($r = 0.30$). Interestingly, the students with higher grit scores tended to have higher GPAs but lower SAT scores than their less gritty peers, suggesting perhaps that what students lack in tested achievement they can make up for in grit or, alternatively, that students who score higher on tests are also more able to achieve high grades without as much dependence on grit. One should be cautious in drawing conclusions from these findings, however. The average SAT score of students in the University of Pennsylvania study was 1415, a score achieved by less than 4 percent of SAT test-takers

nationally (Duckworth, Peterson, Matthews, & Kelly, 2007). It is unclear if the relationship they observed between grit and grades would hold with a more heterogeneous student population in a less elite context.

In the University of Pennsylvania study, grit was measured during the fall term and students reported their cumulative GPA at the same time; thus, the relationship between these measures could have been overstated if students' college performance at that time point influenced their self-reports of grit. Students who knew they were doing well in school (as evidenced by their grades) may have rated themselves more favorably as a result of this knowledge, while students who knew they were performing poorly may have rated themselves more harshly when completing the Grit Scale. A study by the same researchers of military cadets at West Point was longitudinal, with new cadets completing the Grit Scale upon entrance to the military academy. A year later, their grit scores were used to predict grades. In the West Point study, the observed relationship between grit and grades was much smaller than at Penn, although still significant ($r = 0.06$), suggesting that while grit measures might correlate highly with current grades, they may not be as strong a predictor of future academic performance (Duckworth, Peterson, Matthews, & Kelly, 2007).

In the West Point study, the researchers also tested the effects of self-control. They found a stronger relationship between grades and self-control (based on student reports on a self-control scale) than between grades and grit ($r = 0.13$ versus $r = 0.06$; Duckworth, Peterson, Matthews, & Kelly, 2007). The Brief Self-Control Scale (BSCS; Tangney, Baumeister, & Boone, 2004) includes items such as, "I am good at resisting temptation," "I have a hard time breaking bad habits," and "I do certain things that are bad for me, if they are fun," to which students respond on a five-point scale from "not at all like me" to "very much like me" (p. 323).

In a similar study of eighth-grade students at a selective magnet school, Duckworth and Seligman (2005) found self-control measures collected in the first semester—including students' self-reports of impulsiveness and self-control, combined with teachers' and parents' reports of students' self-control (e.g., ability to get things done, follow instructions)—added to the prediction of second semester grades beyond test scores and

22

first semester grades alone (Beta = 0.08). They found a very high correlation between reports on students' self-control and grades (0.55 to 0.67), without controlling for prior semester grades. However, while the study used self-control reports from one point in time (semester 1) to predict grades in another point in time (semester 2), the context remained constant across time. At both time points, students were enrolled in the same school and were taking the same classes. This makes it impossible to disentangle the effects of the context on students' performance from the effects of their self-control or the effects of context on their ratings of self-control.

Thus, while there are studies that show relationships between grit or self-control and students' grades, these findings tend to be stronger when both dependent and independent variables are measured concurrently. When grit or self-control is measured before students have engaged in much of the coursework on which their grades are based, these measures show smaller relationships with (subsequent) performance. This suggests that the strong relationships in the cross-sectional analyses may occur because students' perceptions of their grit and self-control may be affected by their concurrent course performance. More research is needed that examines the relationship of various measures of perseverance with performance in a causal way—with perseverance measured prior to enrollment in courses and without questions on the scale that elicit responses that might be influenced by that performance.

Another series of studies that is often cited to emphasize the importance of self-control for academic achievement comes from an experiment conducted by Walter Mischel and colleagues, sometimes referred to as the "marshmallow" experiment (Mischel & Mischel, 1983; Mischel, Shoda, & Peake, 1988; Shoda, Mischel, & Peake, 1990). In this experiment, children at the Stanford University preschool were left alone with one marshmallow after being told they could have two marshmallows if they waited to eat the one until the experimenter returned. Follow-up studies showed a relationship between waiting for the second marshmallow and higher SAT scores many years later (Shoda, Mischel, & Peake, 1990).

While this study has been used to suggest that self-control in early childhood predicts later academic achievement, Mischel and colleagues found that wait time was only associated with later achievement under particular conditions. When the marshmallow was put in plain sight—which made it difficult for children to avoid thinking about it—and when the children were not given strategies for distracting themselves from thinking about the marshmallow, then Mischel saw differences in wait time that were later associated with higher SAT scores. Mischel's interpretation was that children who could wait longer for the second marshmallow were those with stronger cognitive skills; their higher cognitive skills in preschool allowed them to come up with their own means of distracting themselves while in full view of the marshmallow. The fact that they showed higher SAT scores many years later suggests that this interpretation was correct. However, the message from these studies is not necessarily that self-control predicts higher intelligence but that higher intelligence may make it easier to show self-control.

While the experiment does not provide evidence that self-control leads to better test scores independent of the effects of students' initial intelligence levels, it does provide evidence that whether children exhibit self-control depends on *context* (e.g., whether the marshmallow is in plain sight or not), and on whether the children are given *strategies* that allow them to complete a task successfully (i.e., distraction strategies provided by the experimenter), as well as on children's *cognitive skills* (i.e., whether they can come up with ways to distract themselves). Thus, while students may have different innate levels of perseverance as a personal trait, the degree to which they demonstrate *behavior* that appears perseverant depends on the context they are in and the skills and strategies that they possess, all of which can alter the difficulty level of the task in front of them.

Is Academic Perseverance Malleable?

To a large extent, the malleability of academic perseverance depends on how one defines perseverance. There is a great deal of evidence that students' persistence at tasks, and the degree to which they exhibit self-discipline, changes over time and in different situations. A person who appears perseverant in a particular setting with a particular task might appear unmotivated or halfhearted in another setting with another task. Moreover, changes in classroom context or in the psychological condition of students have been associated with an increase in persistent effort by students. This suggests that perseverance is malleable and responsive to context.

The concept of grit, however, was designed to be consistent across time and context. Duckworth and colleagues suggest that grit behaves like an inherent character trait—in other words, that it is fairly stable over time—and perhaps is most fruitfully understood in the context of the "Big Five" personality traits. Over the past several decades, personality psychologists have come to general agreement on grouping the myriad human psychological characteristics into five universal personality traits, each of which is expressed along a spectrum (such as introversion to extroversion). One of the Big Five—*Conscientiousness*—is the only personality trait that consistently shows a relationship to academic performance. In a meta-analysis, Porporat (2009) found the size of the effect of Conscientiousness on academic performance to be similar to the size of the effect of intelligence on academic performance. While Conscientiousness increases across the lifespan as individuals mature, psychologists generally agree that Conscientiousness is a "fixed trait," meaning that there is little evidence that interventions or environment can substantially change this aspect of a person's basic nature (Srivastava, John, Gosling, & Potter, 2003). Duckworth and colleagues (2007) suggest that grit should also be understood as a stable personality trait—perhaps a mistakenly overlooked facet of Conscientiousness. This does not mean that it is impossible to change a person's grittiness but rather that doing so would be difficult. Duckworth's current work focuses on how to intentionally cultivate grit and self-control, but to date there is little conclusive research showing grit to be a malleable factor.

Do the research and theory behind the concept of "grit" mean that teachers cannot change the degree to which students persist at challenging tasks in their classrooms? No. Even if one's innate tendency to persevere is hard to change, there is ample evidence that people can change the intensity, direction, and duration of their behaviors *despite* their personalities. In other words, whether or not a student has a gritty personality, he can learn to change the quality of his behavior—in effect to *act* perseverant even if that is not in his core nature (McCrae & Costa, 1994; Roberts & Del Vecchio, 2000).

Second, our focus here is on *academic* perseverance rather than perseverance in some general sense. When we make this distinction, the answer to the question of malleability in a given context becomes a resounding "yes." There is significant empirical evidence that students demonstrate different amounts of perseverance at academic tasks under differing conditions, supporting the idea that academic perseverance as a behavior in a specific context is highly malleable. The research suggests that, while there may be little return to trying to make students more gritty as a way of being (i.e., in ways that would carry over to all aspects of their lives at all times and across contexts), students can be influenced to demonstrate perseverant behaviors—such as persisting at academic tasks, seeing big projects through to completion, and buckling down when schoolwork gets hard—in response to certain classroom contexts and under particular psychological conditions.

What Is the Role of Classroom Context in Shaping Academic Perseverance?

In questioning what prevents many students from working hard in school, Dweck, Walton, and Cohen (2011) ask, "Is it something about [the students] or is it something about school?" (p. 2). While there are aspects of student characteristics that affect perseverance, as shown by the research on grit, overall the evidence suggests it mostly may be something about the school. The degree to which students persevere at academic tasks is quite responsive to changes in school and classroom context, although the effect of classrooms on perseverance works indirectly; in other words, classrooms make an impact on something else that then influences a student's perseverance.

The findings from the Mischel "marshmallow" study described earlier show that context plays a large role in whether children exhibit behaviors that may be viewed as impulsive or contrary to short-term goals. In the experiment, when the marshmallow was *shielded from sight* or the subjects were *given strategies* to avoid thinking about the desired object, children were less likely to act in an impulsive manner by taking the single marshmallow. This turns out to be very similar to the findings from research about the classroom antecedents of academic perseverance. Classroom contexts that are

24

structured to support students' success at assigned tasks and that provide students with strategies to make the tasks easier are likely to increase students' perseverance and persistence in completing those tasks.

One way classroom contexts might affect academic perseverance is by influencing students' academic mindsets (classroom context → academic mindsets → academic perseverance). Think, for example, of a persistent and ambitious high school student who works hard to get to college, where she opts to take calculus in her freshman year. Her college instructor does a poor job of explaining the course material and grades harshly on quizzes, causing the student much anxiety. Her attempt to get help during the instructor's office hours ends with him denigrating her intelligence. After failing her second quiz in a row, she sees no way to be successful and drops the course. Despite the innate tenacity that got her to college in the first place, she gave up on calculus when, in a particular context, she thought it was futile to keep trying. The context in which this student tried to learn calculus gave rise to a mindset that she could not succeed, which affected her ability to persevere in that context.

Another way that classroom context can affect academic perseverance is by giving students opportunities to develop metacognitive and self-regulatory strategies. Where teachers share strategies with students that help them be more effective in their learning and allow them to more fully engage in academic tasks, students are more likely to persist despite difficulty. By building students' repertoire of learning strategies, classroom teachers can indirectly increase students' perseverance because they see a payoff from their efforts (classroom context → learning strategy → academic perseverance).

There is cross-sectional research that suggests a strong relationship between learning strategies and perseverant behavior. Bembenutty and Karabenick (1998) looked specifically at the relationship between what they called "academic delay of gratification" and various learning strategies. College students completed a series of items in which they had to choose between two activities, one that would contribute to academic success in a specific class and another that would provide more immediate pleasurable returns (e.g., "Go to a favorite concert, play, or sporting event and study less for this course even though it may mean getting a lower grade

on an exam you will take tomorrow," or "Stay home and study to increase your chances of getting a higher grade" p. 333). The researchers found that students' reported use of metacognitive strategies such as planning, monitoring, and self-regulation was associated with increased likelihood to delay gratification and choose the academic task (r = 0.49). They found similarly strong relationships between academic delay of gratification and a host of other learning strategies (e.g., managing one's time and study environment, r = 0.62; effort regulation, r = 0.58; and cognitive strategies such as rehearsal, r = 0.42 and elaboration, r = 0.38).

In short, psychological research suggests that classroom contexts shape students' academic mindsets, which in turn affect their academic perseverance within that context. Likewise, classrooms can provide students with opportunities to develop learning strategies which have also been shown to increase students' academic perseverance.

Are There Clear, Actionable Strategies for Developing Academic Perseverance as Part of Classroom Practice?

If classrooms can support positive academic mindsets and help students build effective learning strategies, then classrooms could contribute significantly to increasing students' perseverance in completing school assignments and hence to improving their academic performance. Two potential classroom strategies for influencing academic perseverance are either to "teach" perseverance directly (changing the student) or to influence perseverance indirectly through other mechanisms (changing the context). First we explore strategies for increasing perseverant academic behavior by teaching these behaviors directly, and then we look at ways to increase perseverance indirectly by changing the context in which students learn.

Direct instruction around perseverance is most often seen with students with identified behavioral disabilities. Some psychological interventions are designed to improve particular aspects of perseverance for these students by teaching them behaviors associated with impulse control and persistence. Unfortunately, there is little rigorous research examining the long-term effectiveness of such interventions. Often, existing studies do not include a control group and only examine short-term outcomes—such as improvements that are observed at the end of the intervention. Rarely is there long-term evidence of their effectiveness, even six months after treatment. Most of the research on these interventions has been conducted with elementary-aged children, and there is little work studying effectiveness at the high school or college level. There is also little research that examines the effectiveness of these interventions on different types of populations, including nonclinical versus clinical populations, such as students with and without ADHD (Pelham & Fabiano, 2008; Durlak, Furhrman, & Lampman, 1991; van de Weil, Matthys, Cohen-Kettenis, & van Engeland, 2002). Thus, there is an insufficient research base on which to recommend these types of strategies.

A second approach to increasing students' academic perseverance focuses on changing school or classroom contexts in ways that would indirectly influence academic perseverance. As described previously, the literature suggests two distinct pathways: supporting positive academic mindsets and helping students develop effective learning strategies.

There is clear research evidence that students' mindsets have strong effects on their demonstration of perseverant behaviors such as persistence at difficult tasks. When students value the work they are doing, feel a sense of belonging in the classroom context in which they are working, feel capable of succeeding, and believe they will master challenging material with effort, they are much more likely to engage in difficult work and see it through to completion. Dweck, Walton, and Cohen (2011) explicitly suggest that the ways to improve academic tenacity are through interventions aimed at changing students' mindsets directly or by establishing classroom conditions that support the development of positive mindsets. When teachers can present tasks in ways that make success seem attainable, and when they provide students with the support and tools to be successful, students are more likely to engage and persist in those tasks (Dweck, Walton, & Cohen, 2011). What is less clear is whether these effects are lasting and transferable, e.g., whether—post such interventions— students would continue to behave in a tenacious manner if put in a different context. Nonetheless, the evidence is strong that context-specific

interventions that increase academic perseverance can have clear payoffs in terms of improved academic performance within the targeted context.

Lastly, teachers may be able to increase academic perseverance by changing their instructional practice in ways that help students develop and practice effective learning strategies. While more research is needed to show a causal link between teaching learning strategies and students' perseverance in completing assignments, theory and correlational evidence strongly suggest it is an important mechanism. A continued discussion of the relationship between academic perseverance and other noncognitive factors is presented in Chapter 5 (Academic Mindsets) and Chapter 6 (Learning Strategies), along with a more detailed description of the classroom contexts that have been shown to contribute to building academic perseverance.

Would Changing Perseverance Significantly Narrow Achievement Gaps?

It is unclear from the empirical literature whether improving students' academic perseverance would narrow achievement gaps by race/ethnicity. Much of the research tying academic perseverance to student performance has been conducted on high-achieving students at elite institutions (Duckworth, Peterson, Matthews, & Kelly, 2007; Duckworth & Seligman, 2005, 2006). In a population of high-achieving, college-bound eighth-graders, Duckworth and Seligman (2006) did show a gender gap in self-discipline, with girls rated higher than boys in self-discipline by their teachers and parents as well as in their own self-reports. As a result of these differences in self-control, over the course of a year, girls spent roughly twice as much time on homework on average as boys. They found further that this gender difference in self-discipline explained about half of the gender difference in students' grades. However, this work is limited in scope in that self-discipline was measured concurrently with grades—potentially biasing the measurement and not allowing for causal inference—and it was conducted on a select group of already high-achieving students.

Bembenutty and Karabenick (1998) also looked at gender differences in academic delay of gratification in their study of college students. While girls showed higher mean levels of academic delay of gratification than boys, these differences were not statistically significant. The two studies taken together provide suggestive evidence that differences in self-discipline might underlie some of the gender gap in academic achievement, although much more work needs to be done in this area.

There is less research on racial/ethnic differences in academic perseverance. The two biggest racial groups in the Duckworth and Seligman study (2006) were White and African American students, comprising 55 percent and 32 percent of the sample, respectively, but the authors did not report differences in self-discipline by race. Bembenutty and Karabenick (1998) did report racial/ethnic comparisons by grouping White versus non-White students and found academic delay of gratification was significantly higher for non-White students (p < 0.05). This would not explain differences in achievement where White students outperform non-Whites. The broader research evidence on this point is mixed, with varying reports of higher levels of delay of gratification among Whites versus African Americans (Ward, Banks, & Wilson, 1991). There is a need for more research that shows whether there are consistent differences in academic perseverance among different subgroups of students. More longitudinal research and causal studies are needed to determine whether attempts to improve academic perseverance would be likely to improve academic outcomes for all subgroups of students.

Summary of Research on Academic Perseverance

A challenge of studying **Academic Perseverance** is that it is only evident through students' academic behaviors, and the research often conflates students' innate tendency to be perseverant with the actual behavior of doing work. Another complexity arises from how academic perseverance is defined and measured. On one hand, evidence suggests that grit is fairly stable as an individual trait. However, other work clearly shows that students are more likely to exhibit academic perseverance in contexts that promote positive mindsets or when they have the strategies to successfully manage classroom tasks.

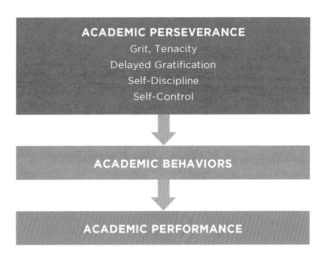

Academic perseverance describes a quality of student engagement in success-oriented academic behaviors and attitudes that is empirically associated with increases in student grades. As such, increasing students' academic perseverance is appealing as a goal for both education policy and classroom practice. However, an isolated focus on academic perseverance as a thing unto itself may well distract reformers from attending to student mindsets and the development of learning strategies that appear to be crucial to supporting students' academic perseverance. As a field, we do not know how to make people innately grittier in a way that transfers across contexts. But the evidence suggests that finding ways to support positive academic mindsets can help students persevere in a given context, and that helping students build effective learning strategies is likely to lead students to more easily handle and hence complete difficult tasks.

While academic perseverance shows moderate relationships to student performance in cross-sectional designs (measuring both perseverance and performance at the same point in time), longitudinal studies find more modest relationships, making it difficult to establish evidence of a causal relationship between perseverance and performance. Although perseverance by race or gender have been suggested as an explanation for racial/ethnic or gender differences in student academic performance, there is little research that has examined this directly and no research that has studied it in a way that would allow for more than very modest causal inference.

27

CHAPTER 5

Evidence on Academic Mindsets

Academic Mindsets are beliefs, attitudes, or ways of perceiving oneself in relation to learning and intellectual work that support academic performance. The theory and empirical evidence on academic mindsets draws on a long history of psychological research. Most commonly, this research has involved correlational studies in which researchers administer questionnaires to measure student beliefs or attitudes, observe students performing academic tasks in either clinical experiments or natural classroom settings, and then analyze the relationship between their measurements of psychological factors and students' task performance.

Lately, mindsets have garnered much attention among researchers because several simple, short-term interventions directed at changing student mindsets have been shown to have surprisingly lasting effects on school performance. These studies suggest that "it can be as important to change people's…interpretations of the social world and their place in it—as it is to change the objective environment" of schools and classrooms (Wilson, 2006, p. 1252). The extensive body of research on mindsets further suggests that a psycho-social approach could have major implications for reform efforts aimed at closing racial/ethnic gaps in student performance and educational attainment.

In Chapter 2 we identified four academic mindsets shown to contribute to academic performance, which we express in the first-person from the point of view of a student:

1. I belong in this academic community;
2. My ability and competence grow with my effort;
3. I can succeed at this; and
4. This work has value for me.

As suggested in Chapter 4, each of these four academic mindsets is positively related to persistence at academic tasks. One of the mechanisms by which mindsets improve students' academic performance is by increasing their perseverance. This leads to improved academic behaviors which result in higher grades. We briefly summarize below the way each mindset affects perseverance.

1. I belong in this academic community. A student's sense of belonging in a school or classroom has a strong impact on academic performance (Battistich, Solomon, Kim, Watson, & Schaps, 1995; Cohen & Garcia, 2008; Furrer & Skinner, 2003; Goodenow, 1992; Goodenow & Grady, 1993; McMillan & Chavis, 1986; Ryan & Deci, 2000; Solomon, Watson, Battistich, Schaps, & Delucchi; 1996; Wentzel & Asher, 1995; Wentzel & Caldwell, 1997). Feeling part of a school or classroom community has significant psychological benefits for students and makes them more likely to engage in productive academic behaviors. In an extensive review of research on school belonging, Osterman (2000) concluded that:

> …the experience of belongingness is associated with important psychological processes. Children who experience a sense of relatedness [in school]… perceive themselves to be more competent and autonomous and have higher levels of intrinsic motivation [than students with a low sense of belonging]. They have a stronger sense of identity but are also willing to conform to and adopt established norms and values. These inner resources in turn predict engagement and performance… [Students who experience belongingness] have more positive attitudes toward school, classwork, teachers, and their peers…They invest more of themselves in the learning process (p. 343).

Conversely, "rejection or the sense of exclusion or estrangement from the group is consistently associated with behavioral problems in the classroom (either aggression or withdrawal), lower interest in school, lower achievement, and dropout" (p. 343).

2. My ability and competence grow with my effort. Students who believe they can increase their academic ability by their own effort are more likely to work toward

28

building competence, more likely to be self-motivating and persistent, and more likely to exhibit behaviors associated with higher academic achievement (Cury, Elliott, Da Fonseca, & Moller, 2006; Dweck & Leggett, 1988). In contrast, these researchers found that students who believe their academic ability is fixed and cannot be changed by their own efforts are more likely to be focused on discerning the opinions of others as to their level of ability, less likely to be self-motivating and persistent, and less likely to do well in school.

A closely related line of research draws on attribution theory, exploring students' attributions for success and failure. If students attribute an incident of poor performance to their lack of ability, they tend to withhold further effort when faced with a similar task (Kelley, 1973; Weiner, 1986; Vispoel & Austin, 1995). Conversely, if students attribute low performance to a lack of effort, they are more likely to increase effort on the next try. As Dweck (1975) summarized:

> The manner in which a child views an aversive event, such as failure, determines, in large part, the way in which he reacts to that event. Specifically, if a child believes failure to be a result of his lack of ability or a result of external factors beyond his control, he is unlikely to persist in his efforts. On the other hand, if a child believes failure to be a result of his lack of motivation, he is likely to escalate his effort in an attempt to obtain the goal. (pp. 682-683)

Believing that ability and competence grow with effort is associated with effort attributions. Notably, in the studies above and replicated elsewhere, beliefs about intelligence and attributions for academic success or failure are more strongly associated with school performance than is actual measured ability (i.e., test scores).

3. I can succeed at this. A third mindset that impacts the degree to which students put forth effort and exhibit strong academic behaviors relates to beliefs about the likelihood they will succeed at a given task. Individuals tend to engage in activities that they feel confident in their ability to complete and to avoid those in which they lack such confidence (Bandura, 1986). People's efficacy beliefs (the perception that they will be able to do something successfully) in both in-school and out-of-school

contexts are positively associated with how long they will persevere at a given task, as well as their likelihood to bounce back when faced with adversity (Pajares, 1996). Conversely, when people do not believe they can succeed at something, they are unlikely to put in persistent effort (Oyserman & James, 2009, p. 381). Efficacy beliefs mediate the effect of skills and of other self-beliefs on performance as they impact the level of students' effort, persistence, and perseverance (Bandura, 1986; Bandura & Schunk, 1981; Bouffard-Bouchard, 1990; Lent, Brown, & Larkin, 1984; Pajares, 1996; Schunk & Hanson, 1985). When students believe they are likely to succeed in meeting academic demands in a classroom, they are much more likely to try hard and to persevere in completing academic tasks, even if they find the work challenging or do not experience immediate success. Believing one can be successful is a prerequisite to putting forth sustained effort.

4. This work has value for me. The degree to which students value an academic task strongly influences their choice, persistence, and performance at the task (Atkinson, 1957; Damon, 2008; Eccles et al., 1983; McKnight & Kashdan, 2009; Wigfield, 1994; Wigfield & Eccles, 1992). Learners are naturally motivated to learn when they perceive a task to be inherently interesting (McCombs, 1991, 1993, 1994). Bruner (1960) noted that "interest in the material is the best stimulus to learning" (p. 14). For example, in a small qualitative study, Lee and Anderson (1993) interviewed sixth-grade students while they were engaged in a classroom science activity. The researchers found that students who valued science prior to the activity were more likely to be "thinking beyond the lesson content and engaging in tasks beyond the requirements or expectations of the classroom" (p. 590). When students are interested in a subject or see a connection between academic tasks and their own future goals, students are more likely to expend persistent effort and exhibit academic behaviors that support school success.

In short, when students feel a sense of belonging in a classroom community, believe that their efforts will increase their ability and competence, believe that success is possible and within their control, and see work as interesting or relevant to their lives, they are much more likely to persist at academic tasks despite setbacks and to demonstrate the kinds of academic behaviors that lead to learning and school success. Conversely, when students feel as though they do not belong, are not smart enough, will not be able to succeed, or cannot find relevance in the work at hand, they are much more likely to give up and withdraw from academic work by demonstrating poor academic behaviors which result in low grades.

What Is the Relationship between Academic Mindsets and Academic Performance?

Drawing on this seminal research from the 1980s and 1990s, much newer lines of work involve implementing psycho-social interventions—often brief treatments or short-term programs designed to promote positive student mindsets—and then comparing the academic performance of students who experienced the intervention to a control group that did not. Researchers such as Carol Dweck, Daphna Oyserman, Greg Walton, and their colleagues have used randomized experiments to evaluate the effect of carefully constructed brief treatments focused on students' mindsets and find compelling evidence that these treatments have lasting effects on students' academic performance. Several intervention studies have tested the effect of promoting what researchers call a "growth mindset," wherein students ascribe to the belief: *my ability and competence grow with my effort.* Students with a growth mindset believe that academic ability is changeable rather than being fixed at a particular level, and they tend to attribute their academic performance to the amount of effort they put into their work, rather than to innate ability, luck, or other factors beyond their control.

In an early example of an intervention study targeting students' attributions for academic performance, Wilson and Linville (1982, 1985) showed a video to a group of first-year college students that depicted older students at the same university discussing their initial difficulty in college, expressly making the point that their performance and GPA improved over time. Students in the control group also received a booklet illustrating what claimed to be normative growth in college students' GPA over time. The researchers' goal was to expose the treatment group to the suggestion that academic setbacks upon entering college are common and not indicative of a lack of innate ability

or some other unchangeable factor. The control group saw a video of the same older students discussing their academic interests, with no discussion of their grades or course performance. The entire treatment consisted of reading the booklet with the GPA information and viewing these brief videos. Although groups were randomly selected and looked similar on key variables before the experiment began, one week after the video screenings students in the treatment group outscored control group students on practice GRE questions. A year later, treatment students had higher college GPAs (0.27 grade point difference) and were 80 percent less likely to have dropped out of school than control students (reviewed in Yeager & Walton, 2011). The authors interpret the findings as evidence that students can be influenced to have a growth mindset, and that a growth mindset contributes to lasting improvements in academic performance.

In a study of the same underlying mindset, Aronson, Fried, and Good (2002) had college students write "pen pal" letters and a short speech about the nature of intelligence that were ostensibly being sent to encourage younger students in middle school. In the treatment group, the letter writers were supposed to promote the idea that intelligence is malleable (a growth mindset). In one control group, letter writers were supposed to write about the existence of multiple kinds of intelligence. A second control group did not engage in any letter writing. The researchers found that students in the treatment group had overall college GPAs that were 0.23 grade points higher than the control groups by the end of the following school term, with African American students in the treatment group also reporting more enjoyment of and engagement in school than African American students in either control group.

In another study on growth mindsets, seventh-grade students in a randomized treatment group participated in a weekly 25-minute advisory group for eight sessions in the spring where they learned that intelligence is changeable and that the brain is like a muscle which grows with use. Prior to the intervention, math grades for both groups had been declining over the course of the year. After the intervention, the math grades of students in the treatment group stabilized while the grades of students in the control group continued to decline, for an overall difference between groups of 0.30 grade points by year's end (Blackwell, Trzesniewski, & Dweck, 2007).

In a separate line of work building on expectancy-value theory (*This work has value for me*), Hulleman and Harackiewicz (2009) had ninth-graders write essays each month about weekly topics in science class. Students in the treatment group wrote about how the science topics applied to their lives. Students in the control group wrote summaries of weekly science topics. The researchers found that students in the treatment group who started out with low expectations for success saw sizeable improvements in their grades at the end of the semester relative to the control group (0.80 grade points difference). There was no significant difference in the grades of treated students who already expected to do well. The researchers concluded that interventions that increase the value of academic work for disinterested students can have positive effects on grades, though these interventions are not likely to affect students who are already positively disposed toward a subject.

The results of these various school-based interventions suggest not only that mindsets are important but also that changing students' mindsets can result in improvements in academic performance as measured by grades. This is clearly good news; it is important work that builds on earlier studies of academic mindsets, and it warrants investment in further research. The implications of the intervention studies, however, should be considered somewhat cautiously. To date, much of the intervention research has included small samples in single schools. Moreover, of the many recent reviews of psycho-social intervention research in education, most have been written by the same people who conducted the studies (see Dweck, Walton, & Cohen, 2011; Garica & Cohen, in press; Walton & Dweck, 2009; Walton & Spencer, 2009; Yeager & Walton, 2011). A broader evidence base would strengthen the claims from these authors. It is also unclear how interventions addressing various mindsets fit together: If a group of students was exposed to multiple interventions targeting different mindsets, would the effects be additive? Who is most likely to benefit from which interventions and under what circumstances? While many questions remain to be answered, the intervention evidence to date—particularly in combination with the earlier theoretical and empirical work upon which it is built—continues to

make a strong case that mindsets are an important non-cognitive factor in student academic performance.

Are Academic Mindsets Malleable?

The apparent success of the interventions cited above suggests that mindsets can be changed intentionally. Indeed, many of these studies demonstrate the malleability of the targeted mindset. Of 13 psycho-social intervention studies reviewed by Yeager and Walton (2011), several specifically measure the targeted psychological variables both before and after the intervention; all of these show changes as hypothesized by the researchers as well as expected differences in student performance (Aronson, Fried, & Good, 2002; Study 2 in Blackwell, Trzesniewski, & Dweck, 2007; Cohen et al., 2006; Hulleman & Harackiewicz, 2009; Oyserman, Bybee, & Terry, 2006; Walton & Cohen, 2007, 2011).

For example, in the Hulleman and Harackiewicz (2009) study intended to increase students' valuing of science through personal connection, we know that, of the students who did not expect to do well in science at the beginning of the study, those who wrote about science in connection with their own lives earned higher grades at the end of the course than those who just wrote summaries of science topics. After the intervention, students in the treatment group also had a higher interest in science and were more likely to indicate plans to take science-related courses in the future than were students in the control group. Walton and Cohen (2007, 2011) measured students' sense of belonging after an intervention meant to activate belonging uncertainty in the treatment group. As hypothesized, African American students who received the treatment had a lower "sense of academic fit" in computer science than African American students in the control group. Also, there were no significant differences in sense of belonging between Whites in the treatment and control groups, supporting the researchers' hypothesis that racial group stigmatization would interfere with African American students' sense of belonging in a way that would not be true for White students.

Blackwell, Trzesniewski, and Dweck (2007) provide contrasting examples of studies in which the malleability of mindsets is demonstrated and those in which it is can only be inferred. The researchers conducted a study in which seventh-graders participated in weekly workshops over eight weeks. Treated students learned math study skills as well as learning that the brain is like a muscle that grows with use. Students in the control group learned only the math study skills. In Study 1, psychological variables (students' implicit theories of intelligence and achievement-related beliefs) were only measured once, at the start of seventh grade, and then correlated with later achievement through seventh and eighth grades. In Study 2, after the eight-week intervention in which students in the treatment condition were taught that the brain can grow with use, the researchers tested the understanding of all students (treatment and control) about how the brain works, as well as measuring changes in their attitudes about the nature of intelligence (before and after intervention). They found that treated students changed their understanding of the brain, changed their beliefs about intelligence, and performed better than students in the control group. Unlike Study 1, Study 2 provides strong and direct evidence that mindsets are malleable.

While not all psycho-social intervention studies have taken this last step of including before and after measures of the targeted variable, those that do have shown changes in the targeted mindset in the expected direction as a result of the intervention. Overall, the evidence suggests that academic mindsets are malleable. They change as the result of experimental interventions, and they also respond to contextual conditions in natural classroom settings.

What Is the Role of Classroom Context in Shaping Academic Mindsets?

A long history of research literature suggests that mindsets are a product of the interaction between students and educational contexts, rather than being predetermined characteristics of individual students (Deci, 1992; Hattie, Biggs, & Purdie, 1996; Masten & Coatsworth, 1998; Stipek, 1986; Wang, Haertel, & Wahlberg, 1994; Yair, 2000). In fact, three of the four academic mindsets we have identified explicitly reflect the attitudes or beliefs of a student *in a specific context:* "I belong in *this* academic community," "I can succeed *at this,*" and "*This work* has value for me." The fourth

mindset, "My ability and competence grow with my effort," is likewise either reinforced or refuted by the context in which a student is expending effort to learn.

Classroom conditions have powerful influences on students' feelings of belonging, self-efficacy, and valuation of schoolwork and can also reinforce or undermine a growth mindset. Conditions in the classroom that have been shown to affect students' mindsets include the level of academic challenge and teacher expectations for success (Conchas, 2006; Rosenthal & Jacobson, 1968; Shouse, 1996; Wentzel, 2002); student choice and autonomy in academic work (Stefanou, Perencevich, DiCintio, & Turner, 2004): the clarity and relevance of learning goals (Grant & Dweck, 2003); availability of supports for learning (Gordon & Bridglall, 2006); grading structures and policies (Assessment Reform Group, 2002; Berliner, 1984; Black & Wiliam, 2004; Brookhart, 1994, 2004; Butler & Nisan, 1986; Covington & Müeller, 2001; Crooks, 1988; Harter, Whitesell, & Kowalski, 1992; Kaplan, Peck, & Kaplan, 1997; Weiner, 1979); the nature of the academic tasks students are asked to do (Bridgeland, DiJulio, & Morison, 2006; Eccles & Wigfield, 1995); the type, usefulness, and frequency of feedback on student work (Brookhart, 1994, 2004; Brophy, 1981; Cohen, Steele, & Ross, 1999; Hamre & Pianta, 2005; Harber, 2004; Stipek, 2001); and classroom norms of behavior and level of trust and safety (Bryk & Driscoll, 1988). As a National Research Council study concludes, positive engagement and self-efficacy in any given subject is contingent upon "creat[ing] a set of circumstances in which students take pleasure in learning and come to believe that the information and skills they are being asked to learn are important and meaningful for them and worth their effort, and that they can reasonably expect to be able to learn the material" (National Research Council and the Institute of Medicine, 2004, p. 14).

Research in both psychology and sociology emphasizes the importance of context in shaping an individual's identity and self-efficacy. Within schools and classrooms, students draw upon frames of reference shared with social groups that are important to them to determine how to act and "who to be" in school, which has implications for how they interpret the world of school and for their subsequent academic behavior

(Berger & Luckmann, 1966; Kaplan & Kaplan, 1982). Social context works powerfully with students' social identities to both define and constrain their sense of what is possible (Weick, 1995). The experience of membership in important social groups shapes students' sense of their own capabilities. As Oyserman & Fryberg (2006) explain, "We can become the kind of person that people of our group can become [and] we fear disappointing important groups by failing to attain group norms and standards" (p. 21). If students feel part of a learning community that values academic work, they are much more likely to share this orientation and act accordingly.

However, the need to meet group norms and standards becomes problematic for students for whom membership in particular social groups may be felt to be at odds with academic achievement. To the extent that students identify with a social group for whom academic achievement is not the norm, they may lower expectations for their own academic success to match those perceived as being normative for the group (Harvey, 1963; Harvey & Schroder, 1963). This effect of classrooms on student mindsets is particularly salient for racial/ethnic minority students and has led to a body of research on stereotype threat, which is addressed in **Box 5.1**.

School Transitions

The role of context in shaping students' academic mind sets becomes apparent when looking at what happens when students move from one school context to another (e.g., in the transition to middle school, high school, or college). Students are particularly vulnerable across school transitions, which are associated with declines in both academic performance and students' attitudes toward school (Alspaugh, 1998; Eccles, Lord, & Midgley, 1991; Hagborg, 1992; Harter, Whitesell, & Kowalski, 1992; Neild & Weiss, 1999; Simmons & Blyth, 1987). School transitions make contexts particularly salient, as students enter a new school milieu, have to reorient themselves to new social and academic demands, and have to renegotiate their sense of self, of academic competence, and of belonging in a new and unfamiliar social space. Many of the intervention studies discussed earlier were conducted on students in either the beginning of their first year in college or their entrance to middle

school or junior high (seventh grade). Effective interventions aimed to normalize academic difficulty, bolster students' sense of belonging, or reinforce a growth mindset to inoculate students from declines in performance following a school transition.

One question that arises is whether these interventions would be as effective among students who were not changing schools. Blackwell, Trzesniewski, and Dweck (2007) found no significant correlation between students' theories of intelligence (fixed versus malleable) and their sixth-grade achievement; however in seventh grade (after entering middle school), having a fixed theory of intelligence was highly predictive of lower performance. In interpreting these results, the authors hypothesized about the role of context in activating the salience of particular mindsets: "In a supportive, less failure-prone environment such as elementary school, vulnerable students may be buffered against the consequences of a belief in fixed intelligence. However, when they encounter the challenges of middle school, [the evidence suggests that] these students are less equipped to surmount them" (p. 258). A fixed mindset constrains students from expending effort to adapt to higher intellectual demands because they do not believe that effort will be enough to overcome the limits of their academic ability.

Recursive Effects

Recent intervention research suggests that contexts contribute to what social psychologists call "recursive effects," which can magnify the interaction between contexts and student mindsets by launching this interaction in a positive or negative feedback loop. Consider the example of a ninth-grader who enters high school unsure of his academic ability and worried about finding friends. When he struggles with the problems on his first math assignment and has a hard time finding a lab partner in science class, he interprets these situations as evidence of his intellectual and social shortcomings. These experiences contribute to growing preoccupations with a lack of belonging and ability which then begin to undermine the student's academic performance, leading to further academic difficulties and lack of confidence. Though the student entered high school feeling unsure of himself, his interactions within the high school context and his participation in its routines

BOX 5.1

Stereotype Threat

Stereotypes about minority students' intellectual inferiority are particularly salient in schools and classrooms. Minority students in the U.S. must struggle to disentangle their own personal narratives of ambition and achievement from dominant societal messages about worth, capability, and academic success sent often unintentionally by schools and teachers. A large body of empirical literature suggests that salient societal stereotypes about minorities' alleged intellectual inferiority or indolence can exert a powerful pull—described as *stereotype threat*—on minority students' self-perceptions, attitudes towards learning, and academic performance (Steele, 1997; cf. Steele & Aronson, 1995; Walton & Spencer, 2009; Walton & Cohen, 2007). Minority students' fears of confirming negative stereotypes about their intellectual ability may lead to underperformance on specific tasks or tests, as students' anxiety about stereotypes interferes with their cognitive processing. Over time, this cycle of threat and the frustration of underperformance may give rise to self-doubt and undermine minority students' commitment to education and achievement. Ultimately, such underperformance may well increase racial gaps in academic achievement and attainment. For example, Perry, Steele, & Hilliard (2003) argue that subtle American narratives about Black intellectual inferiority make the messages African American students receive about their academic capabilities seem ambiguous and even untrustworthy. How are students to know, the authors ask, whether a teacher's feedback is a genuine response to their work or a reaction to what they represent in American culture as an African American?

Previous research suggests that uncertainty about the genuineness of feedback—often termed *attributional ambiguity* by psychologists—can be threatening to minority students' identity and performance in academic settings, both when feedback is positive and when it is negative or harshly critical (Mendoza-Denton et al., 2010; cf. Crocker et al., 1991; Mendes et al., 2008). The mistrust created by uncertainty about teachers' feedback can lead students to discount that feedback, to disengage from specific tasks, and, over time, to disidentify with school altogether (Mendoza-Denton et al., 2010; cf. Major & Schmader, 1998; Steele, 1992, 1997; Cohen & Steele, 2002). A number of studies suggest that strong and supportive relationships with teachers can play a critical role in building a foundation of trust and establishing a basis for minority students to develop positive, stable academic identities (Flores-González, 2002). These relationships provide teachers and students with a platform for delivering and receiving critical feedback, linked to messages conveying high expectations, encouragement, and consistent support that can be used to construct a counter-narrative of success and achievement among minority students (Mendoza-Denton et al., 2008; Cohen & Steele, 2002; Perry, Steele, & Hilliard, 2003).

Intervention studies conducted to address the operation of stereotype threat and belonging uncertainty among minority students provide strong evidence that students' self-evaluations and attitudes respond to conditions and cues in the learning environment. Walton and Cohen (2007, 2011) find evidence that interventions that modify conditions aimed at subtly bolstering minority students' sense of belonging in academic environments substantially affect their performance. These findings suggest that many of the critical challenges facing racial and ethnic minority students in the formation of strong, positive mindsets for academic achievement can be alleviated through the careful work of creating supportive contexts that provide consistent and unambiguous messages about minority students' belonging, capability, and value in classrooms and schools.

Messages about belonging, ability, effort, achievement, success, and value (both one's own intrinsic value and the value of one's education)—intended and unintended, explicit and implicit—are at the core of building students' academic mindsets. Teachers and schools participate in creating school and classroom contexts that either foster the development of academic mindsets and strong, positive attitudes towards learning among minority students or thwart the development of these positive mindsets. Perry, Steele, and Hilliard (2003) suggest that adults need to play specific, predictable, and unambiguous roles in redefining both the content and import of the messages minority students receive about the relationships among belonging, ability, effort, success, and, ultimately, value.

34

reinforce his initial self-doubts and lead to increasingly negative mindsets. These mindsets can become self-perpetuating as the student interprets his school experiences in a way that further undermines his self-efficacy and self-confidence. He withdraws effort from his schoolwork, which results in further poor performance. The ongoing interaction between the student and the school context thus creates a recursive, negative loop between academic mindsets, academic behavior, and academic performance.

It is by breaking this self-reinforcing cycle that interventions around mindsets can cause lasting improvements in achievement (Yeager & Walton, 2011). The theory underlying intervention work is that a well-timed intervention can change an adolescent's schooling trajectory by disrupting this recursive process and resetting the student on a more productive cycle where success and positive expectations are mutually reinforcing. Interestingly, many of these psycho-social interventions aim to *change student perceptions and interpretations* of the school and classroom context rather than changing the context itself.

Are There Clear, Actionable Strategies for Developing Academic Mindsets as Part of Classroom Practice?

There is strong evidence that mindsets matter for student performance, growing evidence that mindsets are malleable, and both a theoretical and empirical basis for the importance of context in shaping mindsets. Unfortunately, the research does not directly translate into classroom strategies that teachers can use to support positive mindsets in their students. Even in the case of experimental research that focuses on specific intervention strategies, it is not clear how these experimental strategies might be used more globally to improve educational contexts. Videotaped interviews of older students at a selective university talking about their difficulty in freshman year might be helpful to incoming students who are experiencing daunting academic challenges, but they provide little direction to the university on how best to support students so routine challenges would seem less overwhelming. Thus, a central tension arising from the research on academic mindsets revolves around how

best to apply the research to improve student outcomes.

If we start with the premise that schools and classrooms often do not provide the positive psychological conditions that research shows to be important for building academic mindsets, then we have two potential approaches to address this. One approach would be to change institutional structures and practices so that students' everyday school and classroom experiences promote positive academic mindsets. Another approach would be to leave schools and classrooms as they are, but to use the findings from intervention research to help students achieve positive mindsets and thus inoculate students from potentially unsupportive environments.

This second option may have great appeal. Investing in a short-term intervention program aimed specifically at building or supporting students' academic mindsets seems like an easier route than reforming instructional practice or changing a whole school culture. Further, the research points to a variety of short-term interventions that have evidence of success in school settings—from programs focused on promoting the growth potential of intelligence to interventions for developing students' sense of belonging. Some of these interventions have become the basis of programs available for purchase by teachers or parents. This raises the possibility that investing in an intervention program could be a prudent way to build students' academic mindsets without changing existing school and classroom practices.

While intervention programs that target academic mindsets might benefit students and contribute to improved academic performance, there is also reason for caution in this approach. First, there are a number of very different intervention programs available: How should educators choose among them? The findings from many intervention studies seem to be consistent (the interventions lead to better school performance), but the treatments are quite different across the studies. Which is the right program for a given school? Furthermore, the effects in most of these studies were selective, affecting some students (e.g., African American college students, seventh-grade girls in math) while not having any impact on the performance of other students—suggesting that specific interventions must be tailored to the psycho-social needs of specific groups of students in particular contexts. How can schools accurately assess the needs of their students so as to apply the right intervention to the right subgroup? Would it be cost-effective to invest in multiple interventions that target different mindsets? Would the effects across these programs be additive or redundant?

Second, it is unclear how big the overall payoff to such interventions would be. While the effects of many of these interventions are significant, some are modest; they average on the order of about 0.3 GPA points. Investing in one of these strategies may be insufficient because they might only have a modest, one-time effect on achievement. There is also evidence that the effectiveness of interventions may be compromised if students become aware of their purpose (Sherman, Cohen, Nelson, Nussbaum, Bunyan, & Garcia, 2009). Thus, attempts to implement them as part of the normal course of school may not have the same payoff as the initial intervention under experimental conditions.

Third, relying solely on intervention programs while not addressing the larger psychological conditions embedded in existing school and classroom contexts will necessarily constrain the effects of the intervention. Learning that the brain is like a muscle that grows with effort motivates students to continue working hard to learn despite setbacks or early failures. But this message may lose its persuasive power if a student's school relies largely either on competitive, one-shot summative assessments to evaluate her performance or on other similar practices that reinforce the value of natural ability over persistent work. Likewise, programs designed to increase students' sense of belonging will have limited impact if their teachers do not know their names and do not recognize or address their particular interests or learning needs.

Instead of, or in addition to, relying on intervention programs to change student mindsets, another strategy involves changing institutional structures and practices so that everyday educational experiences lead students to conclude that they belong in school, that they can succeed in their academic work, that their performance will improve with effort, and that their academic work has value. While there is substantial evidence that changing teachers' instructional practices could improve students' academic mindsets, reforming instructional practice can be difficult. Still, improving classroom contexts

would seem likely to have a larger and broader impact on student achievement and achievement gaps than one-time interventions that only can address a limited sample of students. And while interventions might be easier than instructional reforms in the short run, there is much evidence to draw upon in devising actionable classroom strategies.

The National Research Council and Institute of Medicine (2004) summarized decades of research to identify school conditions that promote strong student engagement and positive academic mindsets. These included: presenting students with challenging but achievable tasks; communicating high expectations for student learning and providing supports that allow students to meet these expectations; making evaluation practices clear and fair and providing ample feedback; reinforcing and modeling a commitment to education and being explicit about the value of education to the quality of one's life; providing students with opportunities to exercise autonomy and choice in their academic work; requiring students to use higher-order thinking to compete academic tasks; structuring tasks to emphasize active participation in learning activities rather than passively "receiving" information; emphasizing variety in how material is presented and in the tasks students are asked to do; requiring students to collaborate and interact with one another when learning new material; emphasizing the connection of schoolwork to students' lives and interests and to life outside of school; and encouraging teachers to be fair, supportive, and dedicated to student learning while holding high expectations for student work.

Many of the strategies that promote positive academic mindsets relate directly to classroom practices around grading and feedback on student work. Supporting positive mindsets around self-efficacy requires that teachers be transparent in their grading practices and explicit about how and why different aspects of student work will affect grades (Assessment Reform Group, 2002; Black & Wiliam, 2004). Instructional contexts that provide students with clear learning goals, and assessment practices that provide students with regular feedback on their progress toward those goals, are essential for creating a school or classroom culture where success is perceived as possible (Kellaghan et al., 1996; Marzano, 2000; Popham, 2000; Tyler, 1949; Tyler, 2000). Students also need repeated opportunities to demonstrate their learning. Giving feedback to students on their progress toward a goal becomes irrelevant if the classroom is not structured to provide students additional opportunity to learn and improve their performance. Researchers have also found that specific kinds of feedback are much better than others in promoting positive mindsets. Praising students for their effort or for their choice of strategy supports the development of a growth mindset and reinforces student effort and enjoyment of academic challenge, while praising students for their talent or ability tends to undermine student effort, cause students to be preoccupied with their ability, and lead to a withdrawal from academic challenge (Mueller & Dweck, 1998).

Classrooms that emphasize cooperation and a sense that everyone can achieve the learning goals are much more supportive of self-efficacy and a valuing of academic work than classrooms that emphasize competition and a zero-sum environment where only a limited number of students will earn good grades (Carr & Walton, 2011; Dill & Boykin, 2000; Johnson & Johnson, 2009; Johnson, Maruyama, Johnson, Nelson, & Skon, 1981; Midgley & Urdan, 2001; Roseth, Johnson, & Johnson, 2008; Slavin, 1995). In their review on academic tenacity, Dweck, Walton, and Cohen (2011) document a number of additional school and classroom practices that promote positive mindsets and increase academic tenacity. These include establishing trusting relationships that instill a sense of belonging, holding high expectations for students, and scaffolding challenging work so that students are able to reach high standards.

While research is clear that classroom context shapes student mindsets and that certain teacher strategies support these mindsets, it is difficult to know how to change classrooms on a broad scale without further research based in actual classrooms aimed at helping teachers acquire such strategies. One potentially fruitful place to start may be in exposing middle and high school teachers and college instructors to the research on academic mindsets and helping them understand the mechanisms by which classroom variables can affect student beliefs about themselves and their schoolwork. However, understanding psychological theory does not automatically lead to knowing what to do differently in one's instructional practice. There are few resources available currently that would translate social-psychological theory into classroom-based instructional practices that could be readily employed by teachers in a variety of school settings to support positive academic mindsets.

Would Changing Academic Mindsets Significantly Narrow Achievement Gaps?

A number of interventions targeting mindsets have been shown to reduce gender and racial achievement gaps. Positive academic attitudes and mindsets that support school performance are important for all students, but racial/ethnic minority students are more likely to face contexts with additional, distinctive challenges to the development of positive academic mindsets. A number of the interventions designed to change mindsets demonstrate large effects on racial/ethnic minority students— or on girls, in the case of math and science performance— suggesting that it is particularly critical to pay attention to the ways in which minority status may shape how students view themselves in relationship to a given learning context. Research on stereotype threat, in particular, suggests that racial/ethnic minority students could benefit from greater attention to academic mindsets.

Many psycho-social interventions are specifically designed to inoculate students against the negative effects of stereotype threat, and indeed they show differential effects on minority students. For example, Cohen, Garcia, Purdie-Vaughns, Apfel, and Brzustoski (2009) had African American and White seventh-graders complete brief writing exercises about values that were important to them. Compared to a control group, students in the value-affirmation group had higher grades, with low-performing African American students seeing the biggest increase in grades (0.41 grade points), sustained over two years. In the Walton and Cohen study (2011), first-year African American and White college students were shown videos designed to help them normalize academic difficulties in the transition to college rather than attributing them to their own personal or racial identity. The significant effect was on African American students' grade point average, which was 0.24 grade points higher than that of control group students from sophomore through senior year of college (Walton & Cohen, 2011) and reduced the racial achievement gap by 52 percent.

The same intervention had no significant effect on the grades of White students.

Ultimately, whether a focus on mindsets can narrow current racial/ethnic or gender gaps in academic performance and college degree attainment depends on the size of these gaps relative to the size of the effects of mindset interventions. It also depends on how much of the achievement gap is caused by stereotype threat or other negative mindsets that would differentially harm minority students in the first place. There is evidence that negative mindsets exist among minority students, as well as among girls in math and science; interventions designed to target mindsets are differentially effective for these groups. Additionally, several studies demonstrate a measured difference in mindsets before and after intervention. There is theoretical reason to believe that the size of the effects of these interventions may actually underestimate the negative impact of stereotype threat and other threats to positive academic mindsets for minority students. The interventions in these studies are generally targeted to change students' construals of their academic environments. To the extent that these interventions are not able to fully counteract potentially harmful psychological messages in those environments or that other factors outside of those academic settings (family, peers, larger socio-cultural context) also exert negative pressures on students' academic performance, the effect sizes of these interventions will be lower-bound estimates of the size of racial/ethnic or gender performance gaps.

One limitation for psycho-social interventions targeting college students is that they may come too late to substantially increase the number of minority students who earn college degrees. This is, of course, true for any intervention aimed at college students. The number of minority students who have successfully made it into college already represents roughly half the age-eligible population nationally. In many urban school districts, half the entering ninth-grade class will not even graduate from high school. Of high school graduates, a large number of minority students either do not proceed to college or enroll in two-year colleges that have low rates of degree completion. Although the interventions targeted at changing the mindsets and improving the performance of college students are beneficial for students who make it to college, greater leverage points for reducing gaps in educational attainment would likely focus on students in the middle grades and early in high school.

Summary of Research on Academic Mindsets

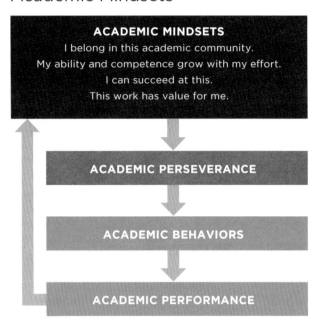

There is strong evidence that mindsets affect student performance. Strong, positive mindsets make students much more likely to engage with academic work, demonstrate positive academic behaviors, and persist despite setbacks. Mindsets are shaped by school and classroom contexts, but they also are malleable at an individual level through experimental interventions. Generally the reported effects from intervention studies are moderate, about 0.2 to 0.3 grade points in size, although these effect sizes may underestimate the actual impact of mindsets on student achievement. It is unclear if mindset interventions transfer across contexts or if students would benefit from more than one intervention. Furthermore, different sets of interventions target different mindsets, and it is unclear whether one intervention would have added value on top of another. While numerous studies have identified specific aspects of classroom context that contribute to strong academic mindsets, a gap persists between research findings and teachers' intentional use of strategies to promote positive student mindsets. Because academic mindsets are so critical to strong student performance, figuring out how to bridge this research/practice gap seems to be a prudent avenue for future work.

CHAPTER 6

Evidence on Learning Strategies

Noncognitive factors are "noncognitive" only insofar as they are not measured directly by cognitive tests. In order to affect learning and academic performance, however, noncognitive factors must engage a student's cognitive processes. The use of **Learning Strategies** is one example of this. As a category, learning strategies encompass several related psychological processes: metacognition, self-regulated learning, time management, and goal setting. Together, these concepts constitute a group of learner-directed strategies, processes, and "study skills" that contribute to academic performance.

Learning strategies have important relationships with other noncognitive factors. Utilizing appropriate learning strategies can make students' academic behaviors more productive and effective, contributing to improved academic performance. As a result, learning strategies tend to increase students' self-efficacy (the *I can succeed at this* mindset), which in turn is related to increased academic perseverance when schoolwork gets challenging. There is also clear evidence that students either with higher self-efficacy or who place a high value on the work they are doing are much more likely to use metacognitive and self-regulatory strategies to engage in learning. Positive academic mindsets drive strategy use, which makes students' academic behaviors more persistent and effective, leading to improved performance. Successful academic performance, in turn, reinforces positive mindsets.

Conversely, a lack of effective learning strategies can contribute to poor academic behaviors and poor performance. Students are less likely to complete homework if they do not know how to organize themselves to get it done, and they are less likely to study for tests if they do not have study strategies that help them review effectively. Not completing homework and not studying have a depressive effect on students' grades. Poor grades in turn undermine positive student mindsets, which then can diminish students' academic perseverance. Likewise, students with low self-efficacy or who place a

low value on the work they are asked to do are much less likely to use metacognitive strategies or to self-regulate their learning; their academic behaviors are less likely to produce learning and quality work, even when students do complete the work. Thus, learning strategies are an important component in a chain of noncognitive factors that shape students' academic performance.

Theorists and researchers have studied many concepts and processes in the broad category of learning strategies over several decades (much of this work is from the 1990s), but there is as yet no single agreed-upon model for what the various components of learning strategies are, how to measure them, or how they affect learning. Across this work, however, there is consensus on a number of points. First, learning strategies involve *metacognition*, defined as an individual's knowledge of and control over his or her cognition (Flavell, 1979; Hacker et al., 2009) or knowing how to monitor one's own understanding (Credé & Kuncel, 2008). Self-regulated learning refers to students' intentional use of metacognitive strategies to achieve learning outcomes (Zimmerman & Schunk, 1989). Rather than being general styles of learning, self-regulated learning and metacognitive strategies are goal-oriented efforts to influence one's own learning behaviors and processes. Students self-regulate their learning by focusing awareness on their thinking and selecting strategies and environments that will be most conducive to learning (Zimmerman, 2001).[4]

A second and related point is that students learn more effectively when they monitor their own learning processes, determine when they are having difficulty, and adjust their behavior and/or strategies to tackle the task at hand (Ford et al., 1998; Pintrich & De Groot, 1990; Winne & Hadwin, 1998; Zimmerman, 2001). Self-regulating learners monitor the process of their learning, ascertain how effectively they are addressing a given learning task, and adjust their efforts accordingly. The process of academic self-regulation can be compared to the thermostat of a furnace, which continually monitors the temperature in a room and responds by adjusting the output of heat (Boekaerts, Zeidner, & Pintrich, 2000). In the absence of this self-regulation, students are apt to give up prematurely, before fully mastering the work at hand, and gain less understanding from the time they do devote to learning.

Researchers also agree that self-regulated learning is a multi-phase process that involves a number of distinct tactics or strategies. These strategies are embedded in behavioral, emotional, cognitive, and executive operations and therefore encompass several simultaneous psychological tasks—which range from invoking judgments about one's personal cognitive abilities, assessing the factors involved in a particular task and how it will influence one's cognition, and selecting cognitive strategies which may facilitate performance (Paris & Winograd, 1990). Winne and Hadwin's (1998) model of self-regulated learning includes four phases. The first phase involves defining or identifying the learning task one is encountering: *What does the task require of me? How is it related to other things I've done? What do I know about this already? How hard will this be?* Once the student defines the task, the second phase involves setting goals in relation to the task and developing plans to reach those goals.[5] This planning aspect entails selecting strategies or tactics to meet the goals the student has set. The second phase also includes deciding on some kind of standard for success: *What will it look like if I've done this successfully?* In Phase 3 the student enacts the tactics/strategies and monitors what happens: *How well is this tactic working? Why didn't it work? Am I as good at this as I thought I was? Should I try a different strategy? Did I learn this well enough?* Phase 4 involves a major reconfiguration of the student's approach to future tasks, based on his or her cumulative experience. As such, Phase 4 only happens occasionally. Winne and colleagues emphasize that these four phases, while conceptually distinct, are recursive or iterative and are only "weakly sequenced" as they occur in the mind of the learner (Winne, Jamieson-Noel, & Muis, 2002).

Other researchers have offered different models of self-regulated learning, but all involve multiple steps or a diverse collection of strategies. Zimmerman (1990) defines self-regulated learning as consisting of

"self-evaluation, organization and transformation, goal setting and planning, information seeking, record keeping, self-monitoring, environmental structuring, giving self-consequences, rehearsing and memorizing, seeking social assistance (peers, teacher, or other adults), and reviewing (notes, books, or tests)" (p. 7). Other researchers differentiate between three categories of learning strategies: *cognitive* strategies such as rehearsal, organization, and elaboration; *metacognitive strategies* such as planning, monitoring, and regulation; and *resource-oriented* strategies such as "creating a favorable learning environment, controlling attention, and sustaining concentration" (cited in Helmke & Schrader, 2001, pp. 13553-13554; see also McKeachie, Pintrich, Lin, & Smith, 1986; Snow & Swanson, 1992; Weinstein & Mayer, 1986). Within these three larger categories, researchers have specified additional levels of elaboration. For example, task awareness, strategy awareness, and performance awareness have been identified as distinct components of metacognitive knowledge (Reynolds, Wade, Trathen, & Lapan, 1989).

While learning strategies generally involve metacognition (monitoring one's understanding) or organizing time and resources (setting aside an hour with the TV turned off in order to read), other strategies are entirely cognitive and have the express purpose of increasing a student's understanding or transferring information into memory. Weinstein and Mayer (1986) identify three such subcategories of cognitive learning strategies: rehearsal strategies, elaboration strategies, and organizational strategies. Generally, the more a learning strategy involves manipulating or organizing material rather than just reviewing it, the more likely it is to result in deep understanding (Weinstein & Mayer, 1986). Winne (1996) describes "deep processing" as the application of studying tactics such as "retrieving concepts and ideas relevant to material currently being studied, monitoring relationships between new information and prior knowledge, assembling propositions into elaborated structures, rehearsing and transforming information into meaningful schemata, and metacognitively monitoring and adapting learning tactics according to the requirements of a task" (Winne, 1996, p. 344, with reference to Schmeck, 1988; Winne, 1985). Note that while these strategies involve both cognitive and metacognitive processes, they fall under the broad umbrella of noncognitive factors because—while they *contribute* to a student's mastery of content knowledge and skills—they are nonetheless *distinct from* knowledge and academic skills as measured by cognitive achievement tests. Still, the category of learning strategies brings us to a particular awareness of the inadequacy of the term *noncognitive*.

For learning strategies to be effective, students must accurately perceive the nature of a task and its demands, and they then must choose and enact appropriate strategies to meet those demands. Learning strategies may often be quite conscious and require focused effort, particularly when tasks are set within a domain of knowledge (e.g., molecular chemistry or the works of Emily Dickinson) that is unfamiliar to a student. As learners move from novice to expert status within a given domain, the selection and use of learning strategies become increasingly automatic (Ericsson & Smith, 1991; Winne, 1996), to the point where students may not even be aware that they are using strategies.[6]

A key component of students' ability to monitor their own thinking is what is called *judgment of learning* (JOL), meaning one's ongoing determination of how much one has learned and whether or not one's level of understanding at any point in time is adequate to the task. This is another important characteristic that distinguishes "expert" learners from less effective students: more accomplished learners know what they know and they know what they have yet to learn; hence, they can tell when they need to put in more effort to accomplish a goal. Researchers studying undergraduates' metacognitive strategies concluded: "One of the critical barriers to success for many students may be their inability to objectively assess their mastery of the academic tasks they are facing" (Isaacson & Fujita, 2006, p. 39), and hence they withdraw effort too soon.

There is considerable evidence that students learn more when they have better metacognitive strategies and use them to facilitate and self-regulate their learning. However, there are several limitations in the research on metacognition and self-regulated learning (see Lennon, 2010). First, most studies are cross-sectional (with evidence collected at only one point in time), yielding little information about how self-regulation may change during adolescence and making it difficult to

link strategy use directly with subsequent academic performance. Of equal importance, "this field of research is still struggling to develop a widely accepted assessment" of self-regulated learning (Lennon, p. 85), with studies using a variety of different instruments to measure similar concepts and a heavy reliance on student self-reports to measure metacognitive strategy use (Winne, Jamieson-Noel, & Muis, 2002). Recently, much of the work on self-regulated learning is within the context of online or computer-assisted instructional delivery (Azevedo, 2005; Hadwin et al., 2007; Winne et al., 2006).

What Is the Relationship Between Learning Strategies and Academic Performance?

Despite the limitations noted above, research shows that students who utilize self-regulation strategies tend to perform better in classroom tasks and activities. Pintrich and DeGroot (1990) examined the self-regulated learning, motivational orientation, and classroom academic performance of 173 seventh-graders in science and English. Using the Motivated Strategies for Learning Questionnaire (MSLQ), a self-report scale[7] that measured student self-efficacy, intrinsic value, test anxiety, self-regulation, and use of learning strategies, they found that students with high self-efficacy used metacognitive strategies more and were more self-regulating than students with low self-efficacy. While self-efficacy and intrinsic value were both strongly associated with self-regulation and strategy use, these motivational variables themselves did not predict performance directly. Rather, it was through students' use of self-regulation strategies that motivational variables affected performance (academic mindsets: self-efficacy/value → learning strategies → academic performance). Self-regulation was the strongest predictor of student performance in both English and science, with significant relationships across a number of measures of achievement (semester grades, as well as grades on seatwork, exams/quizzes, and essays/reports). The authors conclude that teaching students to use self-regulatory strategies in the classroom is vitally important, as the use of such strategies "is essential for academic performance on different types of actual classroom tasks" (p. 38).

McKeachie, Pintrich, Lin, and Smith (1986) tested the validity and reliability of the Motivated Strategies for Learning Questionnaire (MSLQ) to measure college students' motivation and use of learning strategies. They showed strong predictive validity of the motivational subscales and good internal reliability. The motivational scales were related to academic performance in the expected direction, with the learning strategies scales indicating a positive relationship to course grades.

Pokay and Blumenfeld (1990) examined the use over time of both subject-specific strategies and general metacognitive strategies in high school geometry classes. The researchers looked at the relationships among motivation, learning strategies, and academic performance for 283 geometry students in three high schools. At the beginning of the yearlong course, students were asked to complete a questionnaire about their perceptions of ability in math, the value they placed on the class, the likelihood they would be successful in the class, and their use of learning strategies. The authors also obtained students' geometry grades at two points in the course, as well as their prior algebra course grades which were used as a measure of entering math achievement. Early in the course (after proofs were first introduced), the use of specific geometry strategies, metacognitive strategies, and effort management strategies (as well as prior algebra achievement) were all significant predictors of course performance, accounting for 41 percent of the variance in grades. Interestingly, later in the course, metacognitive strategies were the only type of strategy use that predicted grades. These findings suggest that subject-specific strategies may be more useful when a student is learning a new subject such as geometry, and that some level of subject-area proficiency may be necessary before the use of meta-cognitive strategies can lead to successful outcomes.

In another high school study, Zimmerman and Martinez-Pons (1986) identified 14 commonly used self-regulated learning strategies and developed a structured interview tool called the self-regulated learning interview schedule (SRLIS). The SRLIS was used to assess the use of metacognitive strategies of high-achieving and low-achieving tenth-grade students attending a middle-class suburban high school. The researchers found that students' total score for self-regulated learning strategies was the best predictor of both English and math performance (Zimmerman & Martinez-Pons, 1986). Strategy use predicted with 93 percent accuracy students' membership in the high- versus low-achievement groupings.

Finally, researchers explored cross-cultural patterns of high school students' use of self-regulation strategies and their predictive value for academic success. In Australia and Japan, Purdie and Hattie (1996) found within-country patterns of strategy use, such that exchange students from one country were likely to exhibit the strategy use patterns in their host country. However, Japanese students in both countries relied more heavily on memorization strategies than did Australian students. Across both countries, students who viewed learning as understanding (as compared with learning as memorizing, learning as knowledge, or learning as performing academic tasks, for example) used a wider variety of learning strategies and were more likely to engage in strategy use in order to learn, as compared with students with other conceptions of learning (Purdie, Hattie, & Douglas, 1996). In another international study, Nota, Soresi, and Zimmerman (2004) found that Italian students' use of self-regulation strategies in high school—particularly organizing and transforming—predicted their high school course grades as well as their college grades.

Collectively, research provides evidence that knowing and understanding how and when to use learning strategies are associated with higher overall learning and better academic success. These relationships were demonstrated with students in middle grades, high school, and college, across a variety of subject areas, in the United States as well as internationally.

Are Learning Strategies Malleable?

Research supports the idea that metacognitive strategies are malleable and can be developed or learned. Many of the studies reviewed thus far measured strategy use and performance concurrently. While these studies show strong relationships between the two, they leave open the questions of whether learning strategies can be effectively taught and, if so, if teaching such strategies results in improved performance. The research demonstrating malleability uses two common experimental formats. The first involves teaching a skill where

42

students' competence with that skill is measured before and after the skill training. The second measures the aptitude of learners who have been trained in a particular skill against a group of learners who have not had any skill training. While much evidence links learning strategies with better grades, the weakness of many of these studies is their reliance on student self-reports of strategy use or teacher reports on the basis of observable student behavior (Lennon, 2010; Winne, Jamieson-Noel, & Muis, 2002).

Learning strategies can be domain specific, and much of the research focuses on the effects of strategy use on either reading and literacy or mathematics performance. In a meta-analysis by Haller, Childs, and Walberg (1988), the average effect size of metacognitive instruction on reading comprehension across 20 studies was 0.72, a very large effect. Seventh- and eighth-graders benefitted most from metacognitive strategy instruction, which is consistent with Piaget's theory that the formal operational stage of cognitive development occurs around age 12 (Flavell, 1963). During this developmental stage, children begin to think about abstract ideas as well as developing deductive reasoning skills and systematic planning, making it an ideal time to introduce learning strategies that draw upon these processes. The most effective metacognitive strategies were awareness of textual inconsistency and self-questioning to monitor and regulate comprehension. Researchers also found that reading comprehension was greatest when instruction combined the use of several metacognitive strategies rather than focusing on only one or two (Haller, Childs, & Walberg, 1988).

Hattie, Biggs, and Purdie (1996) meta-analyzed 51 studies in reading and other subject areas and found that the average effect sizes due to training in cognitive and metacognitive skills were 0.57 on performance, 0.16 on study skills expertise, and 0.48 on positive affect. While they found memorization techniques to be highly effective for low-level learning tasks such as simple recall of formulas, procedures or facts, learning strategies that aid in higher-level learning require much more from both teacher and learner. Teaching such strategies in the context of the subject-area classroom is much more effective than teaching strategies or study skills in isolation. Findings show training has immediate benefits, but

it is unknown if the positive effects of training persist and transfer to other contexts. For students to be able to transfer learning strategies from one context to another,

the student needs to understand the basis of how the strategy works, when and under what circumstances it is most appropriate, what it requires of the learner; to the extent that this conditional knowledge is properly understood, the strategy may be deployed in contexts "farther" from those in which it was first learned...the further the extent of transfer, the more conditional knowledge and the deeper the content knowledge required. (p. 130)

Dignath et al. (2008) meta-analyzed research investigating whether primary school children could be taught self-regulation skills which would benefit reading, writing, math, science, and self-efficacy. Overall, across 48 studies, self-regulation training produced a weighted effect size of 0.62 on academic performance, using a variety of tactics.

Use of learning strategies in mathematics has also been shown to be malleable. Several studies tested whether math performance benefited from "metacognitive prompting" in which students were asked such questions as "what is this problem about?" or "what steps are you using to solve the problem?" Such cues led to better math performance by prompting students to identify problem structure and task characteristics, draw upon prior knowledge, and evaluate the appropriateness of strategies to solve problems (Butler & Winne, 1995; Kramarski & Gutman, 2006; Kramarski & Zeichner, 2001; Mevarech & Kramarski, 1997; Schoenfeld, 1987; Winne, 1979). There is similar evidence across all major school subjects that learning strategies can be effectively taught (Graham & Harris, 1994; Pressley & Woloshyn, 1995; Wood, Woloshyn, & Willoughby, 1995).

Even if students are not taught learning strategies directly, researchers hypothesize that they learn them anyway. Winne (1996, 1997) refers to this process as "bootstrapping" as students learn to appropriately apply new strategies to learning tasks by trial and error or by observation of the strategy use of others. As reviewed in Chapter 5, students with positive academic mindsets—who value the work or the content area, believe they can succeed in learning it, feel a sense of belonging in a class, and/or believe their efforts will lead to better performance—are more likely to work to acquire strategies to help them learn new material. Regardless of the mechanism whereby new strategies are acquired and applied, there is clear evidence that learning strategies are malleable and can be taught or otherwise developed in students from preschool to college and across a wide range of subjects.

A limitation of the research on learning strategies is its reliance on self-reporting to determine the effectiveness of metacognitive skills training. In any given study, researchers cannot be sure whether metacognitive strategies have actually been "learned" and put to use or if students are simply telling researchers what they think they are supposed to say, based on the content of the training. Conversely, there is evidence that strategy use becomes increasingly automatic as students develop expertise, meaning that students use strategies without being consciously aware that they are using them (Ericsson & Smith, 1991; McKoon & Ratcliff, 1992; Rabinowitz & McAuley, 1990; Schoenfeld, 1985; Winne, 1996). This, too, can confound research based on student self-report of strategy use.

Some of the research is further limited by not specifically addressing student motivation to engage in the strategy use being studied. Researchers often make the assumption that students will be motivated and see the value of participating in the additional tasks and putting forth the additional effort required to utilize strategies to improve learning. A long line of research has shown a strong relationship between student motivation (e.g., academic mindsets) and strategy use, and attention to this relationship is sometimes missing from experimental studies of learning strategies.

What Is the Role of Classrooms in the Development of Learning Strategies?

The development of students' self-regulation and metacognitive strategies is crucial if schools are to teach adolescents to become effective learners. Students can improve their learning by paying attention to their thinking as they read, write, and solve problems. Many metacognitive strategies are subject-specific, meaning

that strategies that help one learn math may be different from the strategies one would employ while reading history. Content-area classrooms are therefore primary sites for the development of students' learning strategies.

Beyond being places where the direct teaching of strategies could most beneficially occur, classrooms play another important role in students' use of learning strategies. Across several of the studies reported earlier, researchers found strong relationships between motivational factors and strategy use. As seen in Chapter 5 on academic mindsets, classroom context is a critical factor in the development of positive academic mindsets, which have been shown to have a strong positive relationship to strategy use in learning.

Pintrich and DeGroot (1990) found that seventh-graders' self-efficacy in science and English, as well as the degree to which they valued those subjects, were strongly related to their use of cognitive strategies and self-regulated learning strategies. Likewise, Pokay and Blumenfeld (1990) found that high school students who placed a high value on learning geometry were much more likely to use learning strategies of all kinds in geometry class. This is consistent with Paris, Lipson, and Wixson's (1983) earlier conclusion that it was not enough for students to know about learning strategies; only when students truly valued the work in a class did they voluntarily use strategies they knew about. To the extent that classrooms foster academic mindsets that help students believe that *I can succeed at this* and *This work has value for me*, they play a crucial role in encouraging students' use of learning strategies shown to improve academic performance. Further, teachers can directly teach students how to most effectively learn course material through the use of both subject-specific and more general learning strategies.

Are There Clear, Actionable Strategies for Developing Learning Strategies as Part of Classroom Practice?

All students can benefit from classroom instruction that builds metacognitive skills and learning strategies, such as monitoring, planning, and self-regulating. Self-observation and self-evaluation are critical metacognitive skills that enable students to self-regulate their behaviors and become effective learners (Bandura, 1986; Zimmerman, 1990). When teachers provide timely, on-going feedback through formal and informal assessments (e.g., discussions, papers, or tests), students are better able to understand which strategies worked for them and where they need to improve. Prompting students to complete self-assessments of their performance provides them with opportunities to practice self-reflection and critique of their learning.

Students benefit when they learn subject-specific metacognitive strategies in the context of subject-area learning. Ironically, they are more apt to be able to transfer strategies across contexts when those strategies are first introduced and learned in very specific contexts. (Bransford et al., 2000). For example, Haller et al. (1988) point out that reading comprehension can be taught by engaging metacognitive strategies through a variety of mental activities involving awareness, monitoring, and regulating. One important metacognitive activity associated with reading consists of training students to be aware when they are not comprehending what is being read and then devising strategies to redirect and compensate for poor comprehension. Rereading, backward and forward search strategies, self-questioning, contrasting textual information with prior knowledge, and comparing main ideas with each other and with details from the text are all examples of learning strategies that may facilitate better understanding while reading.

Another effective instructional practice for teachers is to encourage students to talk about their thinking processes when planning out an academic task. Blakey and Spence (1990) offer the strategy of paired problem-solving where one student talks through a problem by describing his thinking processes while his partner listens and asks questions to help clarify thinking. Similarly, in reciprocal teaching (Palincsar, 1986), a "dialog between teacher and students that involves summarization of the text, question generation, clarification, and predictions about what will next occur in the passage" promotes enhanced learning through the direct teaching of these metacognitive strategies (p. 188). Other strategies enlist teachers to model for students their thinking process while engaged in a task (a "Think Aloud") which in turn provides students with the necessary language to talk about their own thinking processes.

Advances in technology and curriculum development are providing opportunities for teachers to take a more active role in promoting and teaching learning strategies, as reviewed by Bransford et al. (2000). For instance, White and Fredericksen (1998) used an innovative software tool called the Thinker Tools Inquiry Curriculum when teaching physics to typical seventh-, eighth-, and ninth-grade students in urban public middle schools. This is a physics curriculum which allows students to perform virtual physics experiments and compare their results with experiments performed using actual objects. The curriculum encourages students to use a metacognitive approach by highlighting the inquiry cycle and bringing awareness to students' own process of investigation, with time to reflect on their questions and the inquiries of others. Students learn not only about physics but also about processes of inquiry.

In one study, younger students who participated in Thinker Tools outperformed older students taking a traditional physics curriculum. Despite their younger age and lower pretest scores, the Thinker Tools participants (in grades seven through nine) scored higher than traditional physics students in grades 11 and 12 on qualitative problems in which they were asked to apply the basic principles of Newtonian mechanics to real-world situations. By using "an inquiry-oriented, model-based, constructivist approach to science education" that emphasizes metacognitive skills, Thinker Tools "appears to make science interesting and accessible to a wider range of students than is possible with traditional approaches" (White & Fredericksen, 1998, pp. 90-91, as quoted in Bransford et al., 2000, p. 217).

Teachers can use instructional strategies that promote self-regulation without technological aides. For instance, planning and time management are improved when students keep a detailed log of their use of time for one week and use the log to plan their future use of study time (Weinstein & Mayer, 1986). Researchers have also found that if students visualize completing their homework and intentionally think about ways to make it more challenging, it increases the likelihood that they will finish their work and be more deeply engaged in it (Snow, Corno, & Jackson, 1996). Researchers at the University of Victoria in British Columbia teach an on-campus course for college freshmen called "Learning Strategies for University Success," designed to help students develop a toolkit of strategies to learn more effectively and overcome academic challenges in all of their other university courses. A key part of the learning strategies course involves identifying the kinds of challenges one is encountering and then applying appropriate strategies to move forward in learning.

Duckworth, Grant, Loew, Oettingen, and Gollwitzer (2011) tested an intervention on high school students preparing for the PSAT exam using "mental contrasting" and "implementation intentions," two self-regulation strategies previously shown to improve goal commitment and goal attainment in adults. Mental contrasting involves juxtaposing one's vision for a desired future with the constraints or obstacles that might impede reaching one's goals. Implementation intentions refer to the identification of action steps to achieve one's goals, in the form of if-then statements: "if I encounter this obstacle, then I will take these steps." In the Duckworth et al. intervention, 66 students completed written exercises in May of tenth grade regarding the PSAT exam they planned to take the following October. Everyone answered some preliminary questions about their goals for the PSAT and their intentions to use practice tests to prepare for the exam over the summer. Students in the treatment group wrote more extensively about visualizing the successful completion of their goals for completing practice tests and identified foreseeable challenges to their test-preparation plans. Treated students also developed "if-then plans" which involved identifying specific action steps for how they would respond to the challenges they anticipated in completing their summer study goals. Students in the control group wrote about influential people or events in their lives. The May writing intervention took less than an hour total. In July students each received a PSAT practice booklet in the mail, which was collected immediately after completion of the PSAT exam in October. In analyzing the results of the intervention, researchers found that students in the treatment group had completed over 60 percent more practice items over the summer than students in the control group. The authors conclude that

the present investigation suggests that adolescents can learn relatively simple self-regulation

strategies that dramatically improve their ability to attain long-term academic goals. Teachers and schools may therefore consider whether their missions should extend to modelling and instructing students directly in optimal self-regulatory strategies, as well as offering structured opportunities to practice them. (Duckworth et al., 2011, p. 24)

Teaching adolescents to become learners depends in large part on the identification of effective strategies that teachers can share with students to help them achieve their academic goals.

Beyond what we learn from research, practitioners are also a source for classroom practices designed to increase students' awareness and use of learning strategies. In the July 19, 2011, online issue of *Education Week Teacher*, middle school teacher Cossondra George offered teachers a variety of instructional strategies to help students "become responsible for their own learning" by explicitly modeling techniques for notetaking, reading, and studying. George had suggestions for demonstrating literacy techniques in class such as previewing reading passages and restating main ideas in one's own words; modeling how to take notes using a sample passage and giving students time to take notes in groups and compare strategies; encouraging students to set personal learning goals and dedicating time in class to reviewing progress toward those goals on a regular basis; and showing students different approaches to studying for tests, including using note cards to quiz themselves, making up test questions for one another, or playing review games. George also encouraged teachers to advise students to set aside small chunks of study time several days in a row rather than cramming the night before a test. All of these suggested instructional practices are consistent with the research on learning strategies.

Would Changing Students' Use of Learning Strategies Significantly Narrow Achievement Gaps?

There was very little evidence across studies about measured differences in learning strategies by race/ethnicity or gender. None of the research we reviewed reported collecting or analyzing data about students' race or ethnicity. While several studies included gender in their analysis, only the study of high school geometry students by Pokay and Blumenfeld (1990) reported differences in strategy use by gender. Girls used more learning strategies than boys, particularly early in the geometry course. The researchers suggest that this difference in strategy use could account for the finding that boys with low math self-concepts earned lower grades than girls with low math self-concepts, controlling for prior achievement. However, boys with high math self-concepts outperformed girls with high math self-concepts, leading the researchers to conclude that perhaps motivational factors "may be more facilitative for boys' achievement, whereas strategy use may be more facilitative for girls' achievement" (p. 48).

Further research is necessary to see if these conclusions are borne out. As with the other categories of noncognitive factors, the lack of research evidence does not mean that there are no differences in learning strategy knowledge or use by race or gender. Rather, this is a significantly under-investigated area about which we currently know very little. Hopefully future studies will examine these questions directly.

Summary of Research on Learning Strategies

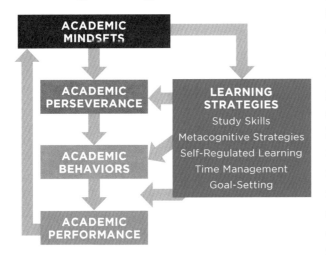

We know that academic behaviors are the most proximal lever for improving student academic performance: better attendance, more studying, and higher homework completion rates would go a long way in improving students' grades. The evidence suggests that using appropriate learning strategies makes each of those academic

behaviors more effective, resulting in deeper learning and higher performance. The use of effective metacognitive and self-regulation strategies may lead students to more actively engage in strong academic behaviors. After all, students are likely to spend more time studying, doing homework, and coming to class if they feel that engaging in such behaviors will lead to academic success. While much of the research is correlational rather than causal, there is a clear link between the use of learning strategies and academic performance.

Research also shows that students who place a high value on the work in a class and who believe they will be successful at it are much more likely to use metacognitive and self-regulated learning strategies when doing that work. Academic mindsets and use of learning strategies have a strong and consistent positive relationship across a wide variety of studies in several different subject areas with students in middle grades, high school, and college. This suggests that classrooms are important both as sites for the explicit teaching of learning strategies and as contexts that set motivational conditions for learning and strategy use.

We found numerous examples of short-term studies designed to evaluate the effectiveness of particular programs or the teaching of specific strategies, usually involving researchers specifying the strategies they wanted to test. However, we could not find any studies of teachers' "natural practice" in developing students' learning strategies or of the effectiveness of existing practice across grade levels and academic subjects. We also found little longitudinal research on any potential long-term effects of learning strategy use on student motivation and academic performance. This is surprising, given the important role of learning strategies in facilitating student understanding of course material and improving students' grades. The learning strategies course at the University of Victoria is the only formalized example we found of explicit instruction in learning strategies designed to improve student performance across subject areas.

CHAPTER 7

Evidence on Social Skills

Social behaviors or **Social Skills** have been linked to academic performance in elementary, middle, and high school, although the preponderance of this research is at the elementary grade level, with a particular focus on primary grades (DiPerna & Elliott, 1999; Feshbach & Feshbach, 1987; Green, Forehand, Beck, & Vosk, 1980; Gresham & Elliott, 1990; Lambert & Nicholl, 1977; Wentzel, 1991). The effect of social skills or behaviors on academic performance is often unclear from the literature. Most studies of social skills come from a broader field of research on social and emotional learning.[8] Gresham & Elliott (1990) give an expansive definition of social skills as "socially acceptable learned behaviors that enable a person to interact effectively with others and to avoid socially unacceptable responses" (p. 1). Such skills include cooperation, assertion, responsibility, empathy, and self-control (Malecki & Elliott, 2002). The Collaborative for Academic, Social, and Emotional Learning (CASEL) lists five "social-emotional learning core competencies" of self-management, self-awareness, social awareness, relationship skills, and responsible decision-making. Examples of ways students demonstrate responsible decision-making include "studying and completing their homework and [using] problem-solving and relationship skills to overcome obstacles" (Greenberg et al., 2003, p. 470). Given the overlap of social behaviors, mindsets, and academic behaviors in much of this work, it is difficult to extract the "social skills" components from other noncognitive factors in this body of research. For the purposes of our review, where research focused on social skills in combination with other factors, we tried to isolate the findings on social skills. However, because studies tend to confound social skills with other variables, we were not able to always isolate the effects of social skills from other noncognitive factors.

What Is the Relationship Between Social Skills and Academic Performance?

There is evidence that work on students' social-emotional skills can have positive effects on school performance but, again, most of this research examines other noncognitive factors in combination with social skills. In a longitudinal study following students through grades one, three, and six and at age 16, researchers found that "socio-emotional adjustment in school" was predictive of achievement test scores at every time point (Teo, Carlson, Mathieu, Egeland, & Sroufe, 1996). Much of the work done in the area of social skills training programs focuses on younger children (pre-K and elementary grades) and often measures results in terms of improved behavior rather than measures of academic performance (Bierman, 1986; Bierman & Furman, 1984; Bierman, Miller, & Stabb, 1987; Coie & Krehbiel, 1984; Ladd, 1981). CASEL published a review of research on 80 programs focused on "social and emotional learning" (SEL), only 20 of which even considered academic outcomes; others were directed toward substance abuse prevention, violence prevention, healthy sexual development, and overall promotion of health (Collaborative for Academic, Social, and Emotional Learning, 2003).

A recent meta-analysis of school-based interventions for enhancing social and emotional learning in students from kindergarten to high school concluded that there were positive effects of social-emotional interventions on academic achievement (Durlak et al., 2011). They found that, in the 35 studies that included academic achievement measures, SEL interventions had an average effect size of 0.33 on student grades and 0.27 on achievement test scores, the latter translating to a percentile difference of 11 percent. Grades only improved in studies where classroom teachers were responsible for delivering the intervention (as opposed to delivery by nonschool personnel). Unfortunately,

48

this analysis cannot disentangle the effect of "social skills" from myriad other social-emotional development concepts. Search terms used to identify relevant studies for Durlak and colleagues' meta-analysis included: *social and emotional learning, competence, assets, health promotion, prevention, positive youth development, social skills, self-esteem, empathy, emotional intelligence, problem-solving, conflict resolution, coping,* and *stress reduction,* and studies qualified for inclusion if they targeted the development of at least one of these skills (Durlak et al., 2011, pp. 408-409).

One theory behind social-emotional learning is that the effects on academic performance are largely indirect, enacted through students' behaviors in the classroom. In other words, if one could develop students' competencies in the areas of self-awareness, self-management, social awareness, relationship skills, and responsible decision-making, then students would engage in more positive social behaviors and have fewer problems with misconduct and less emotional distress, resulting in more engagement in the classroom and hence better test scores and grades (Collaborative for Academic, Social, and Emotional Learning, 2003; Greenberg et al., 2003). Therefore, social skills may improve learning by enhancing social interaction that gives rise to learning (Vygotsy, 1978; Bandura, 1997) or may minimize disruptions to learning and thus have an indirect effect on students' grades (social skills → learning → grades).

Alternatively, it could be that teachers value pro-social behavior; they reward "good" social behavior directly with higher grades while penalizing behavioral interruptions with lower grades (social skills → grades). Indeed, studies of classroom grading practices show that teachers often do include student behavior as a factor when calculating grades. In one study of 307 middle and high school teachers, 37 percent reported including student behavior in their grades (Cross & Frary, 1999). In another study of district and school grading policies, while only 11 percent of school board and district documents specifically mentioned student behavior and attitude as a criterion in grading, 21 percent of school-level documents in those same districts acknowledged behavior and attitude as a factor considered in students' grades (Austin & McCann, 1992). This suggests that social skills may improve student performance not because they

improve learning, but because they are sometimes considered directly in the calculation of students' grades.

Evidence from elementary and middle school suggests that social skills increase academic performance because they allow students to participate productively in classroom activities that foster learning. Slavin's work (1995) on the positive associations between cooperative learning and academic achievement would contribute to this idea. Likewise, Wentzel (1993) found that prosocial behavior (e.g., helping, sharing, and cooperating) and antisocial behavior (e.g., breaking rules and fighting) of sixth- and seventh-grade students (n = 423) each significantly and independently predicted GPA, although only prosocial behavior predicted achievement test scores. In a study of both positive social skills and problem behaviors in third- and fourth-graders in an urban Massachusetts district, Malecki and Elliott (2002) found that student social skills were positively correlated with concurrent grades, while problem behaviors were negatively correlated with concurrent grades. Positive social skills also predicted future academic performance. The study's findings affirmed earlier research by Wentzel (1991) that social skills acted as "academic enablers in school environments" for the elementary students they studied (Malecki & Elliott, p. 18). Wentzel (1993) found that most of the positive effects of social skills on grades were mediated by academic behaviors. She suggested that students who exhibit positive social skills in the classroom (e.g., cooperation or willingness to follow rules) would likely finish schoolwork as expected by their teachers.

A serious limitation of the studies showing a link between social skills and academic performance is that almost all are correlational rather than causal, meaning that measures of social skills and academic performance are taken at the same time. They generally do not provide evidence of the direction of the association between social skills and achievement: Do positive social skills contribute to increased learning, while problem behaviors decrease learning? Or does academic success contribute to positive social and academic behaviors in school, while academic difficulty contributes to problem behaviors? It is likely that social skills and academic performance are mutually reinforcing, but current research does not answer these questions definitely.

Most of the work showing relationships between social skills and grades was done at the elementary school level. Perhaps social skills have a weak direct relationship with course grades in high schools because most high school classrooms tend to minimize the social and cooperative aspects of learning. In contexts where individuals must work collaboratively in problem-solving teams, social skills may be more directly related to performance. Longitudinal studies at the middle school and high school levels are needed if we are to better understand the potential effects of social skills on academic performance over time and the mechanisms whereby social skills may impact grades.

Are Social Skills Malleable?

There is extensive research on social skills training programs that shows they are generally effective interventions, although the methodological strength of these studies varies (Quinn, Kavale, Mathur, Rutherford, & Forness, 1999; Beelmann, Pfingsten, & Losel, 1994; Coleman, Pfeiffer, & Oakland, 1992; Boyle & Hassett-Walker, 2008; McGinnis & Goldstein, 1997). Many of these programs address skill deficits of elementary school aged children, and effect sizes generally vary as a function of the extensiveness and scope of the particular program. Programs that are led by well-trained professionals are more likely to produce change, and outcomes are greater for normal populations of children than children who exhibit clinically significant deficits. Intervention programs address a range of outcomes, which include problem-solving skills training, interpersonal relationship development, coping skills enhancement, and aggression replacement training. Those programs that draw upon behavioral skill-building approaches have also been found to lead to more enduring change, compared to those that do not focus on a specific behavioral skill. Programs designed to be implemented on a formal, school-wide level include those aimed to address problem behaviors in students through such approaches as behavior modification (Lee & Axelrod, 2005; Sarafino, 2001), or, more recently, School-wide Positive Behavior Supports (SWPBS) or Positive Behavioral Interventions and Supports (PBIS) programs (Bradshaw, Reinke, Brown, Bevans, & Leaf, 2008). In their meta-analysis of 213 universal,

school-based social-emotional development programs, Durlak et al. (2011) found an average effect size of 0.69 on social-emotional skill performance, indicating that indeed social skills such as emotions recognition, stress management, empathy, problem-solving, or decision-making skills can be intentionally developed through school-based programs.

What Is the Role of Classrooms in Shaping Social Skills?

Schools and classrooms play an important role in shaping students' social skills. Even where educators view poor student social behavior as a property of individual children that has to be addressed, the strategy for changing student behavior often involves implementing school- or classroom-level systems or programs of behavioral supports. Nonetheless, there is often little acknowledgement that school and classroom systems and structures might be implicated as either causing or exacerbating poor social behavior. A review of the What Works Clearinghouse Personal/Social Development outcome domain reveals that the majority of interventions are focused on "character education" at the elementary and middle school levels. The handful of school-based programs—such as Too Good for Violence (Hall & Bacon, 2005), Skills for Adolescence (Eisen, Zellman, & Murray, 2003), and Connect with Kids (Page & D'Agostino, 2005)—that show positive effects on behavior involve scripted curricula intended to be taught by teachers trained specifically by the curriculum developer. These curricula often include role-playing and cooperative learning exercises that promote good classroom citizenship. Research on these programs focuses on behavioral outcomes that are not tied directly to academic performance.

Durlak et al. (2011) emphasize the importance of school and classroom contexts for positive social-emotional functioning. In addition to "person-centered explanations of behavior change," they note that research also demonstrates that interpersonal, instructional, and environmental factors affect students' social behavior and academic performance, including:

...(a) peer and adult norms that convey high expectations and support for academic success, (b) caring teacher-student relationships that foster commitment and bonding to school, (c) engaging teaching approaches such as proactive classroom management and cooperative learning, and (d) safe and orderly environments that encourage and reinforce positive classroom behavior (e.g., Blum & Libbey, 2004; Hamre & Pianta, 2006; Hawkins et al., 2004; Jennings & Greenberg, 2009). It is likely that some combination of improvements in student social-emotional competence, the school environment, teacher practices and expectations, and student-teacher relationships contribute to students' immediate and long-term behavior change (Catalano et al., 2002; Schaps et al., 2004). (Durlak et al., 2011, p. 418)

In reviewing the research on SEL, they note that effective SEL programming fosters students' social-emotional development "through establishing safe, caring learning environments involving peer and family initiatives, improved classroom management and teaching practices, and whole-school community-building activities" (Cook et al., 1999; Hawkins et al., 2004; Schaps, Battistich, & Solomon, 2004), further noting that "together these components promote personal and environmental resources so that students feel valued, experience greater intrinsic motivation to achieve, and develop a broadly applicable set of social-emotional competencies that mediate better academic performance, health-promoting behavior, and citizenship (ref. Greenberg et al., 2003)," (Durlak et al., 2011, p. 407).

Are There Clear, Actionable Strategies for Developing Social Skills as Part of Classroom Practice?

Social and emotional skills programs we reviewed are primarily geared for elementary-aged students or are designed to move students in special education programs into a mainstream or inclusive classroom. In their review of "universal" school-based programs, meaning those designed for all children in a school rather than particular subpopulations of students, Durlak et al. (2011) note such programs generally involve teaching students to process, integrate, and selectively apply social-emotional skills in appropriate ways, given

students' stage of developmental, as well as contextual and cultural norms (Crick & Dodge, 1994; Izard, 2002; Lemerise & Arsenio, 2000). By systematically teaching and modeling SEL skills and giving students opportunities to practice and apply them in a variety of situations, the goal is to encourage students to include SEL skills "as part of their daily repertoire of behaviors (Ladd & Maze, 1983; Weissberg, Caplan, & Sivo, 1989.)" (p. 406).

All the research reviewed here was based on intervention programs designed to develop students' social-emotional competencies which include social skills in addition to other noncognitive factors. Effective training programs involved sequenced step-by-step approaches that actively involved students in skill development over extended periods of time and had clear and explicit goals, and programs were most effective when implemented with fidelity (Bond & Hauf, 2004; Durlak, 1997; Durlak et al., 2011, Dusenbury & Falco, 1995; Gresham, 1995). Unfortunately, this leaves little direction for classroom teachers wanting to support the positive development of social skills in their students outside of a formal program.

Would Changing Social Skills Significantly Narrow Achievement Gaps?

The research cited here gives little indication as to whether changes in students' social skills would narrow racial and/or gender achievement gaps. In attempting to validate their Academic Competence Evaluation Scale (ACES) and its relation to social skills and problem behaviors, DiPerna and Elliott (1999) found differences between White and minority students on teacher-report measures of interpersonal skills, among other measures of academic competence. Overall, minority students were given ratings lower than White students on each of the ACES components, yet further analyses were not able to determine whether the differences were a function of the instrument or of actual sample differences between White and minority students. Malecki and Elliott (2002) found no significant differences between White and minority elementary school students in social skills or problem behaviors at two time points. They noted higher correlations between teacher assessments of social skills and academic competence for White students than minority students. Wentzel (1994) found that White middle school students were perceived to be more prosocial by their peers and teachers and more likely to pursue prosocial and academically responsible goals than African American students. In the same study, girls scored higher than boys in social goal pursuit, social behavior, social acceptance, and perceived support. Attempting to isolate the effects of both prosocial and antisocial behavior, Wenztel (1993) finds a significant negative relationship between antisocial behavior and academic achievement (as measured by GPA), but does not indicate the extent to which this relationship differs significantly by race or gender.

These findings are limited in the conclusions that can be drawn about social skills differences in adolescents. The correlational nature of most research on social skills makes causal interpretation difficult, and in none of these studies do the authors offer interpretations of measured racial/ethnic or gender differences when they found them. Additionally, much of this work looks at social skills in elementary and middle school contexts; it is likely that social skills will manifest differently as young people progress through adolescence and enter high school and college settings that require different ways of interacting with one's environment.

Beyond the difficulty in determining causation, another issue looms large in the discussion of social skills and achievement gaps: the disproportionate number of minority students, and African American males specifically, who experience disciplinary action in school because of behavioral infractions (Gregory, Skiba, & Noguera, 2010). Given the racial and gender disparities in patterns of disciplinary action, it is necessary to consider whether certain aspects of social skills (i.e., antisocial behavior) are interpreted differently for different groups of students. In the report, *America's Youth: Transitions to Adulthood* (2011), the National Center for Education Statistics (NCES) reports that 57 percent of high-school-age African American males had been suspended[9] in 2007, a significantly higher percentage than any other grouping of students by race or gender.

In synthesizing the literature on the "discipline gap" and how it potentially affects the achievement gap, Gregory et al. (2010) point to research that suggests minority students may experience undue

disciplinary action in school. The authors consider several explanations for the disproportionality in discipline patterns, including demographic background information, prior achievement, and differential behavior as possible student-level contributors (Anderson, 1999; Bauer et al., 2008; Brantlinger, 1991; Kuther & Fisher, 1998; McCarthy & Hoge, 1987; Stewart, Schreck, & Simons, 2006; Wallace et al., 2008; Whelage & Rutter, 1986), and differential selection and processing as potential school-level contributors (Skiba et al., 2002; Vavrus & Cole, 2002; Whelage & Rutter, 1986). Overall the literature suggests that race is the most significant of student characteristics that explains the discipline gap. While correlational evidence suggests that exposure to violence and low achievement are also related to the discipline gap, race still remains as a strong predictor. Socio-economic status had little effect, and one study found that African American students in a higher-income suburban school district still were more likely to be suspended (Rausch & Skiba, 2004). Gregory et al. (2010) also highlight research suggesting that schools may be disproportionally responding to antisocial behavior with harsher punishment for minority students than for White students who display similar behavior (McFadden et al., 1992; Skiba et al., 2008; Wallace et al., 2008).

As it stands, further research is needed to disentangle how discipline patterns, antisocial behavior, and social skills are related, and how each affects academic outcomes or contributes to group-based achievement gaps. The correlational evidence available does not either specify the mechanisms through which these factors may affect academic performance or accurately specify causal direction.

Summary of Research on Social Skills

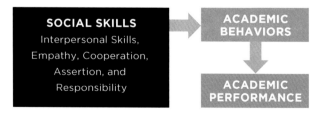

In our model of noncognitive factors, **Social Skills** have the weakest evidence of a direct relationship with grades, in part because measures of social skills

52

or social-emotional competencies overlap extensively with other noncognitive factors. Without more concise boundaries delineating the concept of social skills, the existing evidence cannot distinguish the effects of social skills from other effects. Social skills are important for adolescents as they prepare for future work and interacting in the "real world," but social skills are less utilized in the way classrooms are currently structured where independent tasks and assignments largely determine a student's individual grade. The exception to this may be when the context of the classroom focuses on collaboration and group work; in this situation, stronger social skills may prevail as having a stronger, direct relationship with grades. More research is needed which takes school and classroom context into consideration in examining how social skills may contribute to grades and learning for adolescents across a variety of school settings.

CHAPTER 8

The Role of Noncognitive Factors in School Transitions

Throughout this review, we argue that if research and initiatives around noncognitive factors are to be useable, we need to move beyond evidence from isolated studies to a broader framework that situates the discussion within classrooms and schools. Making the research actionable requires addressing three problems. First, we need to be much more specific about *what matters and why*, which means understanding what noncognitive factors most shape school performance during adolescence and how these factors interact. Second, we need to understand *when noncognitive skills matter*, which means situating the research

evidence within a framework of the cognitive, social, and academic development of adolescents. Are there key developmental points of intervention? When in students' school careers is the development of specific skills, behaviors, attitudes, or strategies most critical in shaping academic performance? And, third, we need to understand *how* critical noncognitive factors can be taught or developed. We illustrate how these issues come together with case studies of three transition points in students' academic careers—the middle grades, the transition to high school, and the transition to college.

54

Noncognitive Factors in the Middle Grades Context

The story of the middle grades illustrates how the elements of our conceptual framework come together—how context influences academic mindsets, and how mindsets shape the development of noncognitive factors. The specific focus on the middle grades highlights the importance of considering students' developmental stage when setting up a context where they are likely to be successful.

As shown in this case study, students' developmental stage interacts with the types of tasks they face to promote or discourage academic mindsets that foster engagement and academic success in school.

In the late 1980s and early 1990s, developmental psychologists studying adolescents focused on understanding a critical phenomenon: for many early adolescents, the middle grades are characterized by decreases in school performance and engagement. These declines are observed both in measures of school performance (e.g., grades) and in attitudinal measures of students' confidence in their academic abilities, motivation, and attitudes toward school (Anderman & Maehr, 1994; Blyth, Simmons, & Carlton-Ford, 1987; Roderick, 1991).

The story that emerged is critical for understanding the role of noncognitive factors—particularly academic perseverance—in declining motivation and school performance during early adolescence. Developmental psychologists have long described cognitive changes in early adolescence, particularly how students begin to have new capacities for formal thought, regulation of behavior, and attributions (e.g., distinguishing between "working hard" and "lacking ability"). How-ever, instructional environments in the middle grades often do not take into account these new capacities or help students develop the academic mindsets and learning strategies they need to successfully take on and persist in new academic demands. As early

adolescents are starting to equate having to work hard with lacking ability, changes in classroom environments and teacher practices begin to emphasize the relative ability of students and to reward students for whom achievement comes easily rather than those who have to put in effort to achieve. At the same time, there is evidence that early adolescence is a key window of opportunity where students are cognitively ready to develop new learning strategies and skills around persistence.

Cognitive Change During Adolescence

Developmental psychologists have long characterized adolescence as a period marked by major developmental shifts in children's cognitive and emotional capacities, including the ability to take the perspectives of others, to self-regulate, and to engage in more formal thought. Piaget characterized adolescents as developing the capacity for "formal operations" and being able to consider multiple dimensions of problems and develop more sophisticated approaches to processing information (Flavell, 1963). It is clear that adolescents begin to "think" differently than they had as children. Until recently, however, the mechanisms for why these changes in cognition occur were not clear. Recent research in neurobiology using brain imaging has filled in these important pieces of the puzzle. The prevailing evidence suggests that the prefrontal cortex matures later than other regions of the brain, developing during adolescence. The prefrontal cortex is the area of the brain that controls "executive functioning" and is linked to social cognition, specifically the ability to see the perspectives of others. In addition, brain synapses—the timing and pathways that the brain uses to process information—also advance significantly during adolescence. Deborah Yurgelun-Todd provides a succinct account of these changes:

> Adolescence is a critical period for maturation of neurobiological processes that underlie higher cognitive functions and social and emotional behavior.... The prefrontal cortex matures later than other regions and its development is paralleled by increased abilities in abstract reasoning, attentional shifting, response inhibition and processing speed. Changes in emotional capacity...are also seen during adolescence.... In summary, brain regions that underlie attention, reward evaluation, affective discrimination, response inhibition and goal-directed behavior undergo structural and functional re-organization throughout late childhood and early adulthood. (Yurgelun-Todd, 2007, abstract)

Thus, as children enter early adolescence they begin to use their brains and process information differently: they think more abstractly, they problem-solve differently, and they have greater capacity to use information to shape behavior. This information processing difference is reflected in adolescent behavior. First, an increased capacity for perspective-taking means that, as students enter the middle grades, adolescents become much more aware of how others see them. The perceptions of others, in turn, begin to shape adolescents' views of themselves to inform their behavior. Second, an increased capacity for decision-making and control means that adolescents become autonomous social actors—they become players in their environment in real ways, making motivation, coping, choices, and relationships ultimately more important to shaping their behavior. Third, the ability for more abstract thought and self-assessment means that adolescents begin to make decisions about motivation and engagement on the basis of feelings of competence, their valuation of the task for both present and future, and their feeling of belonging and social connectedness.

The increasing salience of the distinction between ability and effort during early adolescence is a prime example of how these cognitive shifts converge to influence students' academic performance. Covington (1984) argues that younger children are not able to distinguish between ability and effort. However, as adolescents enter the middle grades, they begin to equate working hard with a lack of ability (e.g., the greater the amount of work required, the less able I must be). Research finds that adolescents' beliefs about learning and the nature of intelligence fundamentally shift to underscore the importance of ability as a latent characteristic (Dweck & Leggett, 1988; Nicholls, 1986, 1989; Nicholls & Miller, 1985). The salience of social comparison heightens a sense of vulnerability and exposure—underscoring a perceived relationship between working hard and a lack of underlying ability. This heightened sense of vulnerability, combined with a growing sense of self-efficacy and a greater recognition of the ability to manipulate their environments through their behavior, underlie adolescents' decisions about whether to engage or withdraw effort in classroom settings. In an effort to not look dumb, adolescents may adopt behaviors and strategies to avoid failures—devaluing challenging tasks, self-handicapping, and withdrawing effort altogether.

In summation, the accelerated development of students' cognition during early adolescence sets the middle grades apart as a key window of opportunity and of risk. On the one hand, during early adolescence, children are developing the capacity to define and establish goals, regulate their behavior, and articulate an increasingly clear sense of themselves as efficacious learners. On the other hand, students' failure to develop strategies and skills during the middle grades can both create skill deficits and reinforce maladaptive patterns of withdrawal and disengagement. Central to addressing declines in school performance is attending to adolescents' conceptions about the nature of intelligence and hard work. Given these changes in students' attribution of efforts, developing approaches to teach students that ability is not fixed would appear to be critical and a high payoff approach to addressing declines in engagement during adolescence as well as improving the degree to which students persevere in academic tasks.

What is critically important about the body of knowledge in the middle grades is that declines in motivation and engagement are not inevitable. Indeed, the general conclusion that arose in this work was that declines in school engagement in this period are largely the product of classroom and school environments. So what goes wrong in the middle grades?

What Goes Wrong: Stage-Development Mismatch in the Middle Grades

In the 1980s, Jacquelynne Eccles and Carol Midgley began a series of seminal studies that situated the problem of declining student motivation and effort during the middle grades within school and classroom contexts (Eccles, Lord, & Midgley, 1991; Eccles & Midgley, 1989; Eccles, Midgley, & Adler, 1984). Eccles and her colleagues argued that changes in middle grades classroom environments and teacher practices, coinciding with developmental changes in adolescent cognition and social behavior, help to explain declines in students' effort, grades, and attachment to school across the transition to middle school. The story is simple: there is a mismatch between the developmental needs of adolescents and the conditions set by teachers within middle grades classrooms. Paradoxically, at a time when adolescents are becoming developmentally ready to assert increasing personal autonomy and assume greater responsibility for their learning, middle grades classrooms become more (not less) restrictive, placing greater emphasis on teacher control and diminishing opportunities for student choice and independence. Second, at a time when early adolescents become increasingly sensitive to social comparison, instructional practices in middle grades classrooms tend to reward ability over effort and highlight social comparison. Third, at a time when adolescents develop the ability to engage in more complex, abstract forms of problem-solving, the academic demand of class assignments declines during the middle grades—schoolwork often becomes less (not more) challenging. Thus, Eccles and her colleagues conclude that declines in school performance largely resulted from a developmental mismatch between the needs of adolescents and their school environment. They summarize the differences observed between elementary and middle school classrooms:

First, junior high school classrooms, as compared with elementary-school classrooms are characterized by a great emphasis on teacher control and discipline, less personal and positive teacher-student relationships, and fewer opportunities for student decision making, choice and self-management... Second, the shift to junior high school is associated with an increase in practices such as whole-class task organization, between-classroom ability grouping and public evaluation of the correctness of work, each of which is likely to encourage the use of social comparison and ability self-assessment leading to a decline in the motivation of all but the most able students. Third, there is evidence that class work during the first year of junior high school requires lower-level cognitive skills than class work at the elementary level. Finally, junior-high-school teachers appear to use a higher standard in judging students' competence and in grading their performance than do elementary school teachers, which leads to a decline in the grades received by most students. (Eccles, Lord, & Midgley, 1991, pp. 533-534)

Research on motivation theory would suggest that these contextual conditions and teacher practices work to undermine rather than promote engagement in learning among early adolescents.

Teaching Adolescents To Be Learners in the Middle Grades

The misfit between the developmental capacities and needs of adolescents and the structures and demands of middle grades classrooms helps us understand the widely observed declines in effort, grades, and school attachment. At a critical moment, adolescent students and teachers are moving farther apart rather than converging in their needs and demands. What we also know, however, is that we can close the gap between students' needs and classroom practices. These studies suggest that the intentional choices adults make about assignments and the structure of middle grades classrooms can set conditions that give students opportunities to develop the academic mindsets and learning strategies that will lead them to persevere towards their goals and act in a persistent manner.

57

Creating successful school and classroom contexts requires that students be developmentally ready to meet new challenges; that learning environments be structured to give students scaffolded opportunities to engage in and wrestle with new challenges; and, finally, that schools and classrooms be intentionally structured to support teachers and students in that work over time.

Evidence from developmental psychology suggests that students entering the middle grades are developmentally ready to tackle and solve a variety of new types of problems; however, extensive research finds that middle grades classrooms provide few meaningful opportunities for students to take ownership of and engage in this work.

Supporting Positive Academic Behaviors in Ninth Grade

While developmental psychologists in the 1990s were studying the transition into middle school and junior high school to explain declines in school engagement during early adolescence, education researchers began to focus attention on the transition to high school as a potentially important point of intervention to address school dropout.

The Transition to High School as a Critical Point of Intervention

In one of the first studies to draw attention to the high school transition, Roderick (1994) found a clear pattern that distinguished the academic trajectory of dropouts from graduates. Students who later dropped out of high school experienced dramatic declines in their grades and attendance—and equally as dramatic increases in course failures—as they moved into high school, regardless of the grade in which they dropped out. Indeed it was largely during normative school transitions that the academic trajectories of dropouts diverged from those of students who would later graduate.

This finding—that a student's capacity to manage the high school transition plays a unique role in predicting school dropout—has now been replicated in multiple studies (Allensworth & Easton, 2007; Felner, Ginter, & Primavera, 1982; Neild, Stoner-Eby, & Furstenberg, 2008; Roderick & Camburn, 1999). In Chicago, CCSR researchers estimate that the link between ninth-grade course failure and eventual dropout is so strong that each additional failed semester course in the first year of high school is associated with a 15 percentage point decrease in the probability of graduating. In other words, failing one full-year course in ninth grade decreases the likelihood of graduating by 30 percentage points (Allensworth & Easton, 2007).

Why would a student's performance in this one period of time be so strongly linked to school dropout? In this case study, we draw on findings from studies of ninth grade at CCSR and research from other places to summarize what we know about why students' school performance declines so significantly, the role of noncognitive factors, and the link to school dropout.

To summarize the story we have assembled, as students start high school, particularly in urban areas, they experience dramatic increases in the complexity of their school environment—in the number of classes and teachers they interact with, in the academic demands of their coursework, and in the size of their school and peer groups. Students must learn to deal with increased independence and more diverse academic demands. They must negotiate and manage relationships with a new set of peers and multiple teachers. This is an important developmental period for the formation of academic behaviors.

The problem is that high school environments are not structured to support the development of those academic behaviors. High school teachers, moreover, are often ill equipped to develop these skills in their students. Thus, at the same time that adolescents are facing new academic and developmental challenges, they experience striking reductions in support and in the monitoring of their performance. Not surprisingly, many students have difficulty managing these new

59

demands. While grade failure in Chicago is not common in the middle grades, ninth-grade failure is widespread. Over half (53 percent) of ninth-graders in Chicago fail at least one semester of a course; 41 percent fail two or more.

Most educators assume that high rates of course failure in ninth grade and declines in students' grades upon entrance to high school are due to students' low skills: the problem, the argument runs, is that students do not have the academic skills to meet the new higher levels of content demands in high school courses. However, the evidence does not support that explanation. Indeed, what is particularly important about the high school transition is that students' grades drop in ninth grade because of dramatic changes in their *academic behaviors*, and this decline occurs among students with strong academic skills as well as among students with weak skills. Because few, if any, teachers are making ninth-grade students come to class and get their work done, they come to view as optional key behaviors like regular attendance, studying, and completing homework. The changes in academic behaviors during the transition to high school are striking. Absences in Chicago nearly triple between eighth and ninth grades, and students' homework completion declines dramatically.

The good news is that these declines in academic behaviors and school performance are largely avoidable. While high schools cannot directly change the entering skills or family background of their students, they can intervene to ensure that students are attending class regularly and they can monitor and intervene quickly when students begin to fall behind in their homework. As we will discuss, efforts in Chicago to improve the proportion of students who are "on-track" to graduation have led to significant increases in the proportion of ninth-graders passing their classes. Evaluations of interventions, such as Talent Development High School's Ninth Grade Success Academies, similarly find that interventions designed to improve support for freshmen are effective in reducing course failure and create impacts that are sustained over time.[10]

Ninth Grade: A Place Where Students "Get Stuck"

School transitions are a challenging time for any adolescent. Studies consistently find that, on average, students' grades, attendance, and attitudes towards school decline following a normative school move— whether they are making the transition to middle school, junior high school, or high school (Blyth, Simmons, & Carlton-Ford, 1983; Crockett, Petersen, Graber, Schulenberg, & Ebata, 1989; Eccles, Lord, & Midgley, 1991; Feldlaufer, Midgley, & Eccles, 1988; Felner, Ginter, & Primvera, 1982; Roderick, 1994; Schulenberg, Asp, & Petersen, 1984; Seidman, LaRue, Aber, Mitchell, & Feinman; Simmons, Black, & Zhou, 1991; Simmons & Blyth, 1987). Urban and minority students are particularly at risk. Urban adolescents' school performance, involvement, and perception of the quality of their school environments decline markedly as they move to middle school and high school (Reyes, Gillock, & Kobus, 1994; Roderick, 1994; Seidman et al., 1994; Simmons, Black, & Zhou, 1991).

Declines in school performance, however, are even more striking in the transition to high school in urban areas because of high rates of absenteeism and course failure. Course failure makes the impact of the ninth-grade transition particularly acute. Failing individual subjects in high school takes on a significance that it did not have in elementary school. In a system where progress is measured by credits accumulated toward graduation, the failure of even one or two classes retards expected progress and represents a large barrier to advancement. Academic failure also undermines school engagement and a sense of belonging, leading students to begin adopting negative school attitudes and behaviors with an eventual downward spiral in performance (Kaplan, Peck, & Kaplan, 1997; Roderick & Camburn, 1996). Just as importantly, without adult intervention, there is little recovery from failure. Students who fail a course in the first semester are at increased risk of failing additional courses the next semester (Roderick & Camburn, 1999).

Lack of credit accumulation is critical to the link between the ninth-grade transition and school dropout. In a review of research on the high school transition, Ruth Neild (2009) characterized ninth grade as a "place in the educational progression where students...are at increased risk of getting stuck" (p. 56). Using data from Philadelphia, Neild and her colleagues found that one-third of dropouts had never accumulated enough credits to move to sophomore standing, even though they had been enrolled in high school for several years. Roderick (1996) documented a similar pattern in Chicago: nearly half (46 percent) of Chicago students who left high school at age of 17 or older left with fewer than five credits (never having completed ninth grade) after being enrolled approximately three years; 70 percent had fewer than 10 credits.

Ninth-Graders with Strong Attendance and Good Grades Are More Likely to Graduate

The importance of ninth-grade course failures was brought into sharp focus with the development of CCSR's on-track indicator. The on-track indicator assesses whether freshmen were "on-track" to graduate on time by having failed no more than one semester of a core subject and having completed enough credits by the end of ninth grade to be promoted to tenth grade.[11] In 2005, 40 percent of CPS first-time freshman were off-track at the end of ninth grade. Ninth grade "on-track" proved to be a powerful leading indicator of graduation. Students who are on-track at the end of ninth grade are nearly four times more likely (81 versus 22 percent) to graduate four years later than students who are off-track.

Importantly, students' course performance in ninth grade has an impact on the likelihood of graduation independent of their academic skill levels. Many educators attribute high rates of course failure to students not being academically ready to manage new high school environments. In this view, course failure is simply a reflection of what skills students bring with them into high school. The evidence, however, is that while academic difficulty in ninth grade is more prevalent among students with low achievement, it is not isolated to these students. **Figure 8.1** presents ninth-grade on-track rates and graduation rates by students' entering achievement. Of students who entered CPS high schools with eighth-grade test scores in the third quartile (roughly equivalent to being in the third quartile on

FIGURE 8.1

Four-Year Graduation Rate by Freshman On-Track Status and Incoming Reading and Mathematics Achievement (Students Entering High School in 2000)

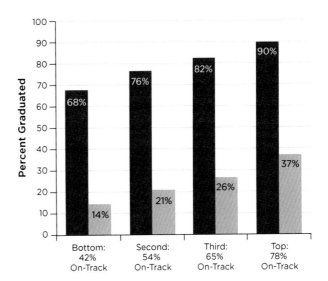

Eighth-Grade Achievement in Quartiles

■ On-Track ■ Off-Track

Source: From Allensworth, E., and Easton, J.Q. (2005). *The on-track indicator as a predictor of high school graduation.* Chicago: University of Chicago Consortium on Chicago School Research. p. 9.

61

national norms), fully 35 percent were off-track at the end of freshman year, and only one-quarter (26 percent) of those who were off-track graduated. Thus, many freshmen who entered high school with test scores at or above national norms had difficulty in the transition, and that difficulty was a significant predictor of whether they would graduate. Conversely, many students with weaker skills managed to be successful freshman year and, if they did so, they had much higher probabilities of graduating than students with higher entering achievement who fell off-track in ninth grade. This does not mean that entering test scores do not matter. Ninth-graders with lower test scores were more likely to be off-track. But the difference in graduation rates between high- and low-achieving students was not nearly as large as the difference in graduation rates between those ninth-graders who were on- and off-track within achievement levels. What this means is that a student's freshman year performance shapes his or her chances of graduating independent of prior achievement (Allensworth & Easton, 2007).[12]

Academic Behaviors, More Than Tested Achievement, Predict Course Failure in Ninth Grade

The pattern in **Figure 8.1** suggests that being on-track in ninth grade is more important than a student's tested achievement in shaping the likelihood of school dropout. In fact, if we try to predict ninth-grade course failure using students' eighth-grade test scores, we only explain 8 percent of the variation in failure rates across students (Allensworth & Easton, 2007). Students' background characteristics—such as gender, race/ethnicity, economic variables, school mobility, age at entry into high school—are also not very predictive of ninth-grade performance. Background characteristics combined with test scores only explain 12 percent of ninth-grade failures (Allensworth & Easton, 2007). Thus, students' academic skills and backgrounds provide only a small indication of whether students will succeed when they enter high school.

The central reason that we cannot predict course failure well is because most students who fail courses in freshman year do not fail because they lack the academic skills to succeed. Rather, students fail courses because they are not attending class, are not doing homework, and are not studying. New evidence from CCSR's more recent high school transition study suggests that the declines in grades and increases in failure between eighth and ninth grades are driven by quite dramatic changes in academic behaviors. This begins with attending class. Students who entered ninth grade in Chicago in the fall of 2008 were absent from school on average for about 10 days when they were in eighth grade. Half of those absences were excused; half were unexcused. The next year, when these students entered ninth grade, their unexcused absences quadrupled. Just one year later, they missed on average 27 days of school, with 21 days being unexcused absences. That is equivalent to missing over five weeks of class.

Students' study habits also decline as they move from eighth to ninth grade. Every two years, CCSR surveys Chicago students in grades six through 10 about their study habits. Because students answer the same questions in middle school and high school, we can compare what they say about how they study in high school (ninth and tenth grades) to what they said when they were in

middle school (seventh and eighth grades). On average, study habits decline by about a fifth of a standard deviation in ninth and tenth grades, compared to seventh and eighth grades (Stevens et al., forthcoming).

After entering high school, students are less likely to report that they: set aside time to do homework, study for tests, do well on schoolwork that isn't interesting, and study before going out with friends.

How important are these changes in attendance and student effort? In Chicago, students' grades in both English and math are almost a half of a grade point lower in ninth grade than they were in eighth grade. **Figure 8.2** presents an analysis of how much of the decline in students' GPA in freshman year can be attributed to changes in academic behavior (Rosenkranz et al., forthcoming). The decline in grades can be explained almost completely by the increase in absences and the decrease in good study habits.

FIGURE 8.2

Reasons for Decline in Grades from Eighth to Ninth Grade

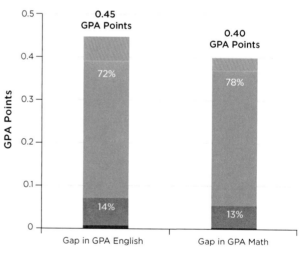

Between Middle Grades and Ninth Grade

Unexplained
Explained by Differences in Absences
Explained by Differences in Study Habits
Explained by Differences in Background and Test Scores

Source: From Rosenkranz, T., de la Torre, M., Allensworth, E., and Stevens, W.D. (Forthcoming). *Free to Fail Research Series: Grades drop when students enter high school.* Chicago: University of Chicago Consortium on Chicago School Research. p. 3.

A Ninth-Grade Problem, Not a High School Readiness Problem

A common response to the problems students encounter in ninth grade is to assume that students are not "ready" for high school; we assume that if we could identify earlier the students who are at risk, we could support them to more successfully navigate the high school transition. Abrupt changes in academic behavior, however, complicate the story: these trends suggest that, contrary to expectations, it is actually extremely difficult to identify which students will struggle in the transition to high school. There is a group of students who show poor academic behaviors in the middle grades, failing at least one course or missing school frequently. Those students who have course failures or very poor attendance in the middle grades are very unlikely to graduate from high school; certainly, we can identify them early because their middle school performance is quite different from that of their peers (Balfanz & Neild, 2006). The problem is that many later dropouts who had difficulty in the transition to high school did not raise warning flags in eighth grade. For example, Balfanz & Neild (2006) found that using middle grade indicators only identifies about 50 percent of eventual dropouts. This means that a substantial portion of dropouts are students who exhibit better academic behaviors in eighth grade; then in a very short time period, they are not demonstrating those behaviors. This highlights the importance of context for students to enact expected academic behaviors. It is the change in environment that leads students to show worse academic behavior when they move to high school.

What is it about the high school environment that leads students to demonstrate worse academic behaviors? Paralleling the middle grades case study, it appears that changes in students' academic behavior reflect both students' struggle to meet developmental challenges and the lack of a developmentally appropriate adult response from schools and teachers—what Eccles has termed "stage-environment" mismatch (Eccles & Midgley, 1989). The change that is most immediately apparent to students when they move to high school is the decline in adult control of their behavior (monitoring) and decreases in academic support. Looking again at changes in Chicago students' responses to surveys

across time (**Figure 8.3**), the same students assessed their relationships with their teachers quite differently in the middle grades and in high school (Johnson et al., forthcoming). The CCSR surveys include measures of the personal attention students receive from teachers, of the level of trust students feel towards their teachers, and of the personal support students feel they receive. The trend across the transition to high school is uniform across all three measures.

FIGURE 8.3

Differences Between Middle Grade and Ninth-Grade Student Perceptions

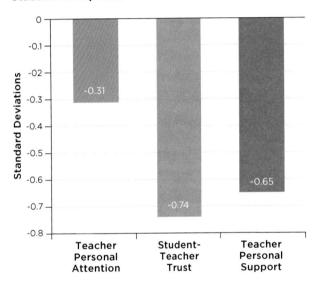

Source: From Johnson, D.W., Stevens, W.D., Allensworth, E., de la Torre, M., Rosenkranz, T., and Pareja, A.S. (Forthcoming). *Free to Fail Research Series: Student-teacher relationships decline at a critical time.* Chicago: University of Chicago Consortium on Chicago School Research. p. 1.

Across the transition to high school, students feel broadly less supported by their teachers. At the same time, ninth-grade students also appear to become aware that there is much less adult monitoring of their behavior occurring in high school. Students can more easily skip class—a behavior largely unheard of in Chicago's K-8 system. These declining measures of teacher attention and support suggest that high school teachers are also much less likely to monitor and control students' effort in class or to make sure they get their homework done. When students begin to struggle with more challenging material in classes, getting help becomes their own responsibility—ninth-grade teachers rarely force students to catch up or seek assistance when they need it, compared to teachers in eighth grade.

63

There are several possible reasons for this decline in support. First, high school teachers are teaching upwards of 150 students; outside of the window of time they have available during class, they may simply have too many students to monitor, to know well, or with whom to develop supportive relationships. Second, Farrington (2008) finds that many teachers strategically withhold support to help students develop independence. High school teachers generally do see ninth grade as a pivotal year—a time when students must learn to become more independent in order to succeed. Many teachers believe that students are most likely to develop the academic behaviors associated with independent learning if teachers refrain from "hand holding" as students struggle to adjust to new institutional demands. By withdrawing support, many teachers believe they are forcing students to "step up"—to take greater responsibility for their own learning—which will allow them to be successful in high school. In essence, students are supposed to learn the importance of academic behaviors by suffering the consequences when they fail to exhibit them.

Unfortunately, a significant portion of students cannot consistently meet these developmental challenges on their own; without adult guidance and support, students have few strategies to draw upon. When students exhibit poor behaviors (skipping class, not completing homework, missing deadlines), the consequences for these behaviors come swiftly in the form of low or failing grades. In Chapter 3, we presented evidence on the direct link between grades and academic behaviors, and here we see that link in action. Grades are not only the most proximal tool teachers have to influence students' academic behaviors; grades are essentially derived from behaviors. If a student does not turn in homework, the homework grade becomes an F.

These patterns can quickly become a vicious cycle: The consequences to students of poor academic behavior may be immediate and costly, but merely suffering these consequences may not help students adapt to their new environment and improve their behaviors. From the student perspective, the work demands of high school can seem overwhelming and the directions or expectations unclear. On top of that, they begin accumulating poor grades despite their efforts. From the teacher perspective, frustration with student behavior is compounded by their own lack of effective strategies to turn things around. Under deteriorating conditions, the threat of failure too often becomes teachers' primary tool for addressing students' poor academic behaviors.

If we step back and consider the research literature, what are the noncognitive factors that most strongly influence academic behaviors? Students who are equipped with effective learning strategies and possess academic mindsets of belonging, relevance, self-efficacy, and the valuing of effort are most likely to exhibit positive behaviors and the academic perseverance to succeed in their courses. Classrooms that build these strategies and support these mindsets are characterized by clear goals and high expectations for student success, the teaching and practice of strategies that help students become effective learners, significant levels of teacher monitoring and support, multiple opportunities for students to achieve success, and an absence of fear of failure.

Ironically, in attempting to help ninth-graders build the independent academic behaviors that are essential for high school success, teachers often end up creating classroom conditions that completely undermine the development of academic mindsets that would support those behaviors. By focusing narrowly on changing student behaviors through punitive grading practices, teachers lose sight of what really matters: creating classroom conditions and employing instructional practices that help students develop positive academic mindsets and learning strategies that research shows will lead to improved academic behaviors.

The Avoidable Failure

Of the three cases we present in this report, the transition to high school is the period where the evidence is strongest about what matters, the link between noncognitive factors (in this case, academic behaviors) and student outcomes is clear, and the connection to the classroom and the day-to-day work of school is evident. We also have strong evidence that schools can influence students' freshman-year performance.

The experiences of two urban school districts—Philadelphia and Chicago—illustrate how intentional programming and supports for incoming freshmen in the transition to high school can make a significant difference in students' ninth-grade performance and

64

can have lasting effects on high school performance and graduation rates. MDRC evaluated the effects of the Talent Development High School Model's Ninth Grade Success Academy in seven low-performing high schools in Philadelphia (Kemple et al., 2005; Kemple & Herlihy, 2004). The Talent Development High School (TDHS) Model was developed in response to national research showing increased failure rates and large declines in attendance and academic performance, particularly for low-income and minority students as they entered high school.

A central feature of the TDHS model is the Ninth Grade Success Academy, designed to combat key problems common to low-performing urban high schools. To address the problem of student anonymity, Ninth Grade Success Academies have their own separate space from the rest of the high school, and teachers and students are grouped in small learning communities to foster closer and more personal relationships among students and adults. To combat low student expectations, all ninth-graders are programmed into rigorous college preparatory courses that meet in 90-minute blocks and have an emphasis on real-world projects that are aligned with the interests of students. To address poor prior preparation of incoming students, TDHS puts students in double-blocked English and math classes to provide them with additional time and support, as well as "catch-up courses" and a "Twilight Academy" as flexible options for students who need either additional focused instruction to prepare them for an upcoming class or who need to make up missing course credits. All ninth-graders also take a Freshman Seminar "designed to prepare students more broadly for the demands of high school" by combining "study skills, personal goal-setting, and social and group skills" (Kemple et al., 2005, p. 23). While these components are not necessarily framed in the language of academic mindsets, the Ninth Grade Success Academies are designed to support students to believe that they belong in the academic community, that the work is relevant, and that they can succeed with effort.

According to a rigorous analysis by MDRC, the seven Talent Development High Schools in Philadelphia "produced substantial gains in attendance, academic course credits earned, and promotion rates during students' first year of high school. These impacts emerged in the first year

of implementation and were reproduced as the model was extended to other schools in the district and as subsequent cohorts of students entered the ninth grade" (Kemple et al., 2005, p. iii). The TDHS schools experienced a 28 percentage point increase in students passing algebra and a 9.5 percentage point increase in the proportion of ninth-graders promoted to tenth grade (Kemple et al., 2005). Matched control high schools, in comparison, showed little improvement. Early evidence also suggests that these ninth-grade improvements were sustained through tenth grade and are correspondingly translating into improvements in high school graduation rates.

CPS took a different approach to supporting incoming students in the transition to high school. Building off the CCSR research about the "on-track indicator" and the importance of students' performance in ninth-grade classes, CPS added schools' "freshman on-track" rates to its accountability metrics and provided data supports to help high schools monitor the performance of its ninth-graders. Using freshman transition programs, "on-track labs," and new watch lists and data tools, CPS high schools began to focus on ensuring that high school freshmen attend school regularly, get appropriate interventions and support, and pass their classes. Between 2007 and 2011, the ninth-grade on-track rates in CPS increased from 57 to 73 percent district-wide, with one quarter of traditional high schools showing improvements of over 20 percentage points. This means that a significantly smaller number of students was failing courses as a result of the additional monitoring and support provided by the high schools. In preliminary analyses of cohort data, it appears that the percentage of students on-track at the end of freshmen year held constant or increased by the end of sophomore year, even though students did not receive additional supports after they became sophomores.

The evidence from both Philadelphia and Chicago suggests that educators can structure school and classroom contexts in ways that wrap developmentally appropriate supports around students as they enter high school, resulting in better academic behaviors in he form of improved attendance and higher rates of homework completion which translate to improved academic performance and a reduction in course failures. The early indications from both cities are that strong supports for students in ninth grade may act as protective factors that carry students forward with better performance throughout high school. There is a strong theoretical basis for this effect. If increased monitoring and support help ninth-graders to develop strong academic behaviors and if a more personal learning environment supports them in building academic mindsets of belonging and self-efficacy, students are likely to demonstrate more persistence in their schoolwork and to earn better grades.

Ninth grade is a crucial point of intervention; as students enter high school they encounter institutions that demand much of them but provide little in the way of appropriate supports, as evidenced by systematic increases in absence and failure, even from students who performed well in eighth grade. Ninth-grade course failure sets up students for further failure. Not only do they face structural barriers in trying to regain missing credits, but the research on noncognitive factors suggests that these experiences may foster negative or counterproductive mindsets as students feel like they do not belong and cannot succeed in high school. Conversely, by coupling interesting and challenging classes with appropriate monitoring and support, there is evidence that high schools can help students build good academic behaviors and positive academic mindsets that may well provide them with a critical foundation that can carry them forward to high school graduation.

The Postsecondary Transition

Research evidence has identified a number of promising strategies for building and sustaining school environments and classroom contexts that support the development of the strong academic behaviors that ninth- and tenth-grade students need to succeed in the transition to high school. However, much less is known about what either high schools or colleges can do to ensure students' success in higher education.

More In, Fewer Out: Educational Attainment in the Twenty-First Century

Put bluntly, too few students attend college, and fewer still complete four-year college degrees. The U.S. is facing a crisis of educational attainment. As U.S. President Barack Obama observed in his 2009 State of the Union address, some three-quarters of the fastest growing occupational sectors in the American economy require more than a high school diploma; yet, barely over half of Americans have the education to qualify for those jobs. Beginning in the last two years, for the first time in U.S. history, American retirees have greater levels of educational attainment than young adults entering the workforce (OECD, 2011). This is, President Obama noted, "a prescription for economic decline."

At the center of this crisis in educational attainment is the college retention puzzle: why do so few students who enroll in college complete their degrees? Over the last two decades, there have been substantial increases in the numbers of minority and first-generation students enrolling in college; however, gaps in college graduation by race and income have remained steady or widened (Bowen, Chingos, & McPherson, 2009). Across all racial/ethnic groups, just over half of students who enroll in college graduate; over the last decade, it has taken college graduates progressively longer (five and six years, in many cases) to complete their degrees

(Bowen, McPherson, & Chingos, 2009). Why has college completion not kept pace with college enrollment? Could noncognitive factors represent part of the solution to the college retention puzzle? This is perhaps the most critical issue on the national education policy agenda. However, despite the urgency of this effort, research evidence remains limited.

Weak Preparation and Declining Financial Aid Only Partially Explain Low College Degree Attainment

The national policy discussion around college retention has generally seized on two explanations of why the U.S. is failing to produce greater numbers of college graduates:

- Weak academic preparation for college coursework, particularly among African American and Latino students; and

- The combination of rising college costs and the declining value of financial assistance (Roderick & Nagaoka, 2008).

While there is clear evidence that prior academic achievement and financial constraints affect college retention, new research strongly suggests that a range of additional factors, including noncognitive factors, plays a critical role in students' postsecondary success. Academic mindsets interventions targeting students' sense of belonging, for example, have shown significant effects on both college retention and grades, However, as a growing number of researchers has begun to recognize, none of these explanations of low attainment accounts for college context. Previous research finds that students with similar levels of academic achievement and college qualifications (e.g., similar grades and test scores) have substantially different college outcomes, largely driven by where they attend college (Allensworth, 2006; Bowen, Chingos, & McPherson, 2009; Roderick, Nagaoka, Coca, & Moeller, 2008).

Colleges are not interchangeable; vast institutional differences exist in how colleges organize and structure the tasks associated with students' academic and social transitions, reflected in the tremendous variation in institutional four-year graduation rates—ranging from over 90 percent of each incoming cohort to under 10 percent. Colleges vary in whether and how they approach and support students' social adjustment, in how they provide academic resources and support, in how (and how much) financial aid is distributed, and in whether and how the campus climate itself is organized to support positive interactions with peers. On the one hand, despite the growing public attention paid to college readiness, there remains relatively little empirical evidence on what precisely it means for students to be "college ready." On the other hand, evidence shows that where students attend college will ultimately determine whether and in what measure their incoming academic achievement and/or noncognitive factors will affect their college persistence. In colleges with low institutional graduation rates (often those that provide few of the developmentally appropriate intellectual and/or social opportunities, challenges, and supports that stretch and grow students), even well-developed noncognitive factors are unlikely to improve students' probability of graduating on time.

How Colleges Organize and Structure the Tasks of Transition Matters

In *Potholes on the Road to College*, CCSR researchers documented the links between CPS students' social capital for college-going, their academic achievement in high school, and their likelihood of enrolling in college (Roderick, Nagaoka, Coca, & Moeller, 2008). That research showed that even highly qualified minority and first-generation college students struggle during the college search and application processes, in large measure because of deep social capital deficits. These students have access to few resources for college-going in their communities, putting them at substantial disadvantage during competitive admissions processes. High-achieving CPS students and others like them, researchers concluded, were especially dependent on the support and direct assistance of high school staff members—primarily counselors and teachers—to focus and refine college searches; to close gaps in college knowledge (Conley, 2007); and particularly to manage the complex process of applying for federal, state, and college scholarships and financial aid. However, while high schools may effectively attenuate the negative impact of social capital deficits in the college choice process, they do not eliminate those deficits as students enter college. Ultimately, college retention is influenced more by the institutional characteristics of colleges than by students' entering characteristics.

Substantial prior research demonstrates that college retention is substantially driven by how colleges organize and structure the tasks associated with students' academic and social integration. Previous studies show that institutional characteristics of colleges are connected with student activities and behaviors that broadly promote social adjustment to campus (e.g., living on campus, attending college full-time, being involved in campus activities, having strong social networks) (Berger & Milem, 1999; Cragg, 2009; Hurtado & Carter, 1997; Oseguera & Rhee, 2009; Pascarella et al., 1986; Ryan, 2004; Scott, Bailey, & Kienzl, 2006; Thomas, 2000; Tinto, 1987; Titus, 2004; Titus, 2006a; Titus, 2006b). Likewise, previous research also connects institutional factors with college retention, including how colleges structure students' interactions with faculty, per-student expenditures on instruction, and student academic support (Arum & Roksa, 2011; Astin, 1993; Berger & Milem, 1999; Bradford et al., 1997; Cragg, 2009; Gansemer-Topf & Schuh, 2006; Nagda et al., 1998; Pascarella et al., 1986; Ryan, 2004; Scott, Bailey, & Kienzl, 2006; Tinto & Goodsell-Love, 1993). How colleges structure students' financial aid packages—particularly whether financial aid is provided in the form of grants or loans—also

68

affects student retention (Bailey & Kienzl, 2006; Blanchfield, 1972; Braunstei, McGrath, & Pescatrice, 2000; Cabera, Nora, & Castaneda, 1992; Cragg, 2009; DesJardins, Ahlburg, & McCall, 1999; Hu & St. John, 2001; Li & Killian, 1999; McDonough & Calderone, 2006; Nora, Barlow, & Crisp, 2006; Oseguera & Rhee, 2009; Somers, 1995; Somers, 1996; St. John et al., 1994). Finally, multiple studies have shown that whether and how colleges structure campus climates to minimize particular challenges minority and/or first-generation college students face related to cultural transitions not experienced by their peers affects college persistence for those students (Astin, 1993; London, 1989; Phelan et al., 1991; Pike & Kuh, 2005; Terenzini et al., 1996; Tierney, 1999; Titus, 2006a).

Noncognitive Factors Matter, But How?

How colleges organize and structure students' experiences on campus affects college retention, but to what extent are the differential effects of institutional characteristics due to student noncognitive factors? What do we know about which noncognitive factors are associated with college retention, and what do we understand about how the college context affects the salience of those factors? Which noncognitive factors matter and how? The research evidence on these questions is surprisingly weak.

College Requires Strong Academic Mindsets and Intellectual Engagement

Previous research suggests somewhat vaguely that in the transition to college, students must become new kinds of learners, not only harnessing a growing body of content knowledge across high school and college courses but also developing and deploying key academic mindsets and learning strategies. In addition to the quality and rigor of students' high school classes, research on the expectations that college faculty hold for students in college courses underscores the importance of developing students' academic mindsets during high school: their beliefs that ability and competence grow with effort; the notion that they can be successful in college coursework; and the conviction that courses are relevant and valuable (Conley, 2003, 2007; Farkas,

2003). Conley (2003, 2005) provides one of the most widely recognizable models of college readiness. He argues for the importance of a broad array of skills and knowledge that students putatively need to succeed in college, variously referred to as "tools" or "habits of mind" (p. 39), described in detail elsewhere as

...critical thinking, analytic thinking and problem solving; an inquisitive nature and interest in taking advantage of what a research university has to offer; willingness to accept critical feedback and to adjust based on such feedback; openness to possible failures from time to time; and the ability and desire to cope with frustrating and ambiguous learning tasks. (Conley, 2003, p. 8)

Conley's work also contrasts the "conceptually oriented curriculum" of colleges with the "content-based curriculum" of high schools, arguing that, in order to succeed at the college level, students must master "interpretation," "thinking skills and habits of mind," "independent work, initiative, sustained effort, inquisitiveness, and attention to detail and quality" (pp. 75-76). Despite the breadth and intuitive appeal of Conley's framing, however, it is critical to note that the intellectual demands and institutional climates students encounter in the transition to college will depend in large measure on where they choose to attend college. In colleges and universities with higher institutional graduation rates—a rough proxy for the quality of the college environment and the social and academic supports available to students there—students are likely to face new and more complex demands from college faculty and their peers. Previous studies suggest that college faculty in these institutions expect and demand a higher level of intellectual engagement from students—one which requires students to cultivate a thoroughgoing inquisitiveness and an engagement with intellectual problems and puzzles without clearly evident solutions (Conley, 2005). Conversely, high school students who enter nonselective four- and two-year colleges may encounter similar or even diminished levels of academic demands as compared to those they faced in high school courses.

Students Also Face Challenges Becoming Integrated Into the Social and Academic Life of College Campuses

In addition to mastering not only new course content but also new ways of learning and engaging with peers, adults, and course materials, prior studies of college departure underscore that students must be prepared to translate existing knowledge and skills into a new context, becoming integrated into the social and institutional life of colleges. For minority and first-generation college students, the transition to the college environment may also represent a first encounter with an unfamiliar and sometimes subtly hostile racial climate. Extensive research in social psychology suggests that minority and first-generation college students experience strong but often imperceptible racial pressures on college campuses, which can undermine minority students' sense of belonging (Yeager & Walton, 2011) and their commitment to obtaining a college degree, undercut their academic behaviors, and even artificially depress their cognitive performance (Steele, 1992, 1997).

Steele argues that racial minorities, particularly African Americans, must compete with the stigma attached to highly racialized images that exist across various social spaces and actively work to perpetuate pre-existing notions of intellectual inferiority. On the one hand, previous research suggests, actively attempting to combat stereotypes about minority intelligence can become an exhausting performance in which one comes to understand that proving one's knowledge in one realm can have no bearing on another; thus, being accepted in one educational setting does not automatically "vouch" for students' skills in the next class setting (Steele, 1992). As a result, over time, minority students may feel a loss of control over their academic performance and a loss of scholarly identity, ultimately resulting in poor academic performance, perhaps particularly among higher-achieving students (Steele, 1992). The direct and indirect effects of such identity threats may ultimately undercut not only minority students' confidence but also their commitment and attachment to the goal of obtaining a college degree, particularly in educational settings where professors fail to convincingly separate academic potential from incoming skill sets (Steele, 1992). Recent research in psychology,

highlighted elsewhere in this report, suggests that isolated, relatively short interventions targeting students' sense of belonging in school can produce significant and lasting effects (Walton & Cohen, 2007; Walton & Spencer, 2009; Yeager & Walton, 2011). This research suggests that the effects of students' self-perceptions— as well as the underlying perceptions themselves—are largely context-dependent. Although promising, this line of research has yet to fully explore how particular dimensions of college context may attenuate or exacerbate the negative effects of stereotype threat and low sense of belonging.

Students' Academic Goals and Sense of Self-Efficacy Modestly Predict College Retention

Beyond the limited evidence linking students' academic mindsets and particularly their sense of belonging with college outcomes, there is also modest empirical support for the notion that students' goals, self-efficacy, and study skills also influence college retention. Robbins et al. (2004) conducted a meta-analysis of 109 studies examining the relationship between noncognitive factors, sorted along nine broad, theoretically determined constructs (Robbins et al., 2004). They found a very modest association between college retention and three noncognitive factors: academic goals, academic self-efficacy, and academic-related skills. Academic goals were measured using constructs including goal commitment, commitment to the goal of college graduation, preference for long-term goals, desire to finish college, and valuing of education. Academic self-efficacy was measured using constructs including academic self-worth, academic self-confidence, course self-efficacy, and degree task and college self-efficacy. Academic related skills were measured using constructs including time management skills, study skills and habits, leadership skills, problem-solving and coping strategies, and communication skills (Robbins et al., 2004, 267). However, beyond the confusing, overlapping array of concepts and terms, findings such as these suggest little about how these factors affect students' college retention prospects and provide no information whatsoever about the malleability of these constructs or their responsiveness to context. While important, these results are little help to policymakers and practitioners seeking to identify appropriate levers for improving students' college persistence and degree attainment.

Other studies, including recent work by the College Board (Schmitt et al., 2011), ACT ENGAGE (Le, Casillas, Robbins, & Langley), and private, for-profit corporations (Gore, Leuwerke, & Metz, 2009) have sought to capitalize on the limited evidence connecting noncognitive factors with college outcomes by developing research-based survey tools to measure high school students' noncognitive skills. Marketed at the intersection of practitioners' concerns about college retention and institutional decision-making surrounding college admissions, these products attempt to transform the limited insights of the existing research base into early indicators of students' college prospects. In these products, information about students' noncognitive factors is viewed as complementing existing information about students' prior academic achievement (e.g., high school GPA and standardized test scores) to give college admissions staff a fuller view of an applicant's potential for success. However, as Schmitt et al. note in a report for the College Board, the incremental validity of the measures of noncognitive factors used is small, and the measures themselves may be especially subject to manipulation by test-takers (e.g., in situations where individual scores might be used in college admissions decisions). These limitations suggest that, despite the interest in tools measuring students' noncognitive preparation for college, there is substantial warrant for skepticism about their validity and broader utility.

Context Matters: College Choice and the Postsecondary Transition

Taken together, the prior research linking noncognitive factors to college outcomes suggests at least three conclusions: first, while there are strong theoretical reasons to believe that noncognitive factors are connected with college outcomes, there is still little empirical research directly exploring these connections, especially between noncognitive factors and college retention. Additionally, research studies have yet to explicitly explore the ways in which the importance of various noncognitive factors examined may

be driven by specific elements of the college context. This first conclusion strongly points up a second: the large body of research on institutional strategies for improving college retention strongly suggests that colleges substantially influence students' experiences and outcomes in the transition to college. However, to this point, the existing research base has not investigated in detail how the institutional contexts of college campuses may influence the relative importance of particular noncognitive factors. In short, while existing literature suggests strongly that noncognitive factors matter in college, we still understand much less about how those factors matter—and how much—depending on where students choose to attend college.

Finally, there is much about the connection between noncognitive factors and college retention that we simply do not know. What empirical evidence exists suggests some connection between students' mindsets, behaviors, and skills, on the one hand, and their outcomes in college on the other—but research has provided far too little useful evidence on what these factors really mean, whether they are in fact amenable to change, and whether they can be manipulated effectively in the high school context. These are not reasons to believe that noncognitive factors do not matter in the transition to college. On the contrary, these are reasons, we argue here, for researchers to double down on the bet that high schools and colleges each have a role to play in setting institutional and classroom-level contexts that foster students' intellectual and noncognitive growth. In one sense, research on the college transition lags far behind what we know about the middle grades and the transition to high school: there is a great deal of ground to be made up in bringing up to speed our understanding of how noncognitive factors matter in the transition to college and what we can do about it.

CHAPTER 9

Interpretive Summary

Leveraging Noncognitive Factors to Improve Student Outcomes

Since the mid-1980s, test score-based accountability has dominated American public education. This movement took on the force of federal law in 2001 with the No Child Left Behind Act, as every state in the country administered standardized tests to measure student and school performance. Ask any teacher, principal, or educational administrator about goals for the year; increasing test scores is the most likely response.

President Obama's first address to Congress signaled a shift in educational priorities. He committed his administration to ending the dropout crisis in the nation's public high schools and ensuring that by 2020 America would once again lead the world in the proportion of its population with college degrees. This shift has brought a host of education policies geared at increasing academic demand: adding graduation requirements, increasing participation in advanced coursework, and setting more rigorous curricular standards. The widespread adoption of the Common Core State Standards reflects an agreement across states to set a higher bar for college and career preparation.

What has not been talked about is that a shift to making high school and college completion our national educational goal requires a corresponding shift in educational policy and practice, *away from a focus on test scores* and toward a new emphasis on developing the cognitive and noncognitive factors that lead students to earn high course grades.

The emerging recognition of the importance of noncognitive factors to young people's long-term success raises new challenges for teachers seeking to prepare their students for college and careers. It also creates a conundrum for educators who have been told to focus on raising test scores, not only for purposes of accountability but also because test scores have been touted as strong indicators of student learning and college readiness. The evidence on the relationship between noncognitive factors and student grades—and between grades and long-term outcomes—challenges this focus on tests. If teachers want their students to be successful—both within their current courses and in their future endeavors—then teachers must attend to students' engagement in class material and their coursework performance, not just their tested performance. To make this shift, educators need to understand how best to help adolescents develop as learners in their classes. This should not be framed as an *additional* task for teachers, though for many it may mean teaching in new ways. By helping students develop the noncognitive skills, strategies, attitudes, and behaviors that are the hallmarks of effective learners, teachers can improve student learning and course performance while also increasing the likelihood that students will be successful in college.

The importance of students' grades—rather than test scores—for later outcomes requires that we better understand how to structure classrooms and schools in ways that improve student effort and performance in the daily tasks of the classroom. Of all the challenges posed by the implementation of the Common Core State Standards, this may be the greatest: if we are truly to be a nation of college-goers, we must not only raise the bar on *what* students learn but we must also leverage an understanding of noncognitive factors to teach adolescents *how* to become effective learners. In the absence of developing students as learners, current reform efforts are unlikely to succeed at increasing students' readiness for college.

This report grew out of the understanding that it is not enough to know that noncognitive factors matter for learning. Researchers from a range of disciplines have provided evidence that such factors are important to students' grades and long-term educational outcomes. However, little work has been done to bring clarity to this wide-ranging evidence, to examine its relevance for practice, or to review actionable strategies for classroom use. Our goal was to develop a coherent and evidence-based framework for considering the role of noncognitive factors in academic performance. We conclude by summarizing the most promising levers for change as well as critical gaps in the knowledge base and in the link between research and practice.

Students Earn High Grades When They Show Perseverance and Strong Academic Behaviors

The best ways to improve students' perseverance and strengthen their academic behaviors is through *academic mindsets* and *learning strategies.* This is the central point emerging from our review. Academic behaviors and perseverance reflect the level of students' engagement in their work— the degree to which they are coming to class, completing assignments on time, participating, studying, trying to master material, taking time to do challenging work, and sticking with a task until it is done well. Students who do these things get higher grades, and students who do not do them struggle academically. This becomes increasingly true as students transition from the middle grades to high school and on to college. Strong academic behaviors and academic perseverance are the noncognitive *outcomes* that teachers want to achieve in developing their students as learners. These are the noncognitive factors most directly associated with good grades.

It is hard to change academic behaviors and academic perseverance directly without addressing academic mindsets and effective learning strategies. Ironically, trying to directly change behaviors and perseverance is not the best lever for improving students' academic performance. The critical levers for improving student grades seem to be through the development of academic mindsets and learning strategies. Academic mindsets strongly influence the degree to which students engage in academic behaviors, persevere at difficult tasks, and employ available learning strategies. In turn, the use of appropriate learning strategies strongly influences the quality and effectiveness of academic behaviors and helps students stick with a task and persevere despite obstacles. Thus, building students' academic mindsets and teaching them appropriate learning strategies are the best ways to improve

academic behaviors and perseverance, which leads to better grades. Unfortunately, these are often areas in which teachers have little training. In the absence of a strong framework that clarifies the role of schools and classrooms in the development of noncognitive factors and a toolbox of strategies to effectively support this development, teachers often attribute differences in students' academic behaviors and perseverance to individual characteristics of their students—something they cannot control.

Unfortunately, teachers often misdiagnose poor academic behaviors and lack of perseverance not as a lack of strategies or a problem with mindsets but as indications that students are not motivated or do not care. Students who are not working hard in school are often diagnosed as being lazy or lacking motivation, with teachers seeing these as personal characteristics that students bring with them to the classroom. The conclusion that follows is this: if students would just work harder and not give up, they would do better in school; their academic performance is poor because either they do not care enough to try or they lack the grit or determination necessary for success.

Our research framework of noncognitive factors sheds a different light on the phenomenon of students who exhibit poor academic behaviors. Perhaps what looks like a lack of caring or persevering could be a student indicating that she is convinced that she cannot do the work. Another student may not have effective strategies for engaging in classroom tasks. Students who cannot see the relevance of a class may have difficulty finding a way to engage in the work. Others may withdraw from participating in classroom activities because they are afraid of public failure or feel ostracized by their peers. In our own research, we find that the vast majority of students want to succeed in school, but many obstacles get in the way of their putting forth effort.

Developing adolescents as learners requires paying attention to students' mindsets, skills, strategies, and behaviors as well as their content knowledge and academic skills. If students are not demonstrating strong academic behaviors, teachers need to be able to determine and address the obstacles that deter their learning. We hope that the framework presented in this report can serve as a tool to diagnose potential underlying causes for weak engagement and poor academic behaviors and to develop strategies for re-engaging students as learners.

School and classroom contexts play a crucial role in shaping these noncognitive factors in individual students. Within a given course, students' sense of belonging, self-efficacy, and interest will be shaped by their experiences in the classroom, their interactions with the teacher and fellow classmates, their prevailing beliefs about their own ability, and the nature of the work they are asked to do. Their endorsement of a growth mindset will be shaped by the structure of learning opportunities and assessment practices, as well as by the messages they receive from teachers that emphasize ability or effort. Likewise, students are not likely to develop learning strategies in the absence either of explicit instruction or classwork that requires the use of such strategies.

It may be most helpful to think about noncognitive factors as properties of the interactions between students and classrooms or school environments. Rather than being helpless in the face of students who lack perseverance and good academic behaviors, teachers set the classroom conditions that strongly shape the nature of students' academic performance. The essential question is not how to change students to improve their behavior but rather how to create contexts that better support students in developing critical attitudes and learning strategies necessary for their academic success. Thus, teaching adolescents to become learners may require educators to shift their own beliefs and practices as well as to build their pedagogical skills and strategies to support student learning in new ways. Academic behaviors and perseverance may need to be thought of as creations of school and classroom contexts rather than as personal qualities that students bring with them to school.

The Role of Noncognitive Factors in Academic Performance: Implications for Research

The role of noncognitive factors in students' academic performance has gained increasing attention from both researchers and practitioners in recent years. While some very interesting and promising work has emerged recently, the state of the research evidence and the development of practice models still lag far behind the

high level of interest. In this review, we were focused primarily on the implications and actionable pathways for teachers and classrooms that emerge from the research evidence. For this reason, we asked a different set of question of the research literature than one might ask in a traditional literature review conducted by an academic in this field. For each noncognitive factor, we asked:

- How is this factor related to academic performance?
- Is this factor malleable?
- What is the role of classroom context in shaping this factor?
- Are there clear, actionable strategies for classroom practice?
- Would changing this factor significantly narrow existing gaps in achievement by gender or race/ethnicity?

With this lens, we saw four major challenges that must be addressed if research on noncognitive factors is going to be useful for educational practice.

1. The need for conceptual clarity. One of the primary challenges to making research accessible to practitioners and relevant to policy is the lack of conceptual clarity among the many noncognitive factors that affect student performance. Much of the research conflates constructs that are conceptually very distinct. For example, work on social-emotional learning has used the demonstration of academic behaviors as indicators of having social-emotional core competencies (e.g., using studying and completing homework as measures of responsible decision-making). Likewise, academic tenacity has been described not only as showing persistence in tasks despite obstacles (the usual connotation of the word *tenacity*) but also as the mindsets that encourage tenacity—such as self-efficacy, sense of belonging, and a growth mindset. However, perseverance, mindsets, and behaviors are each conceptually distinct categories—a student can have a strong sense of self-efficacy but still not participate in a given class, for example. To really understand the mechanisms by which noncognitive factors affect academic performance requires conceptual clarity and a delineation of each step in complex interactive processes.

2. The need for direct evidence. A related shortcoming of some of the existing research is that researchers sometimes use noncognitive factors as a "catch-all" explanation for differences in student achievement without directly identifying or measuring specific factors. Some very influential research merely infers the existence of noncognitive factors when researchers are unable to find a measured cognitive explanation for differences in educational or workforce outcomes across different groups. In Heckman and Rubinstein's (2001) seminal study of the economic returns to a GED, for example, they attribute wage differences between GED recipients and high school graduates to differences in noncognitive skills without directly measuring any noncognitive skill differences or demonstrating their direct relationship to wages. Heckman and Rubinstein acknowledge this, explaining that there are too many different traits subsumed under the name "noncognitive skills" and no one way to measure them all. What they then attribute to differences in "noncognitive skills" is simply the difference in wages between high school graduates and GED recipients that could not be explained by tested achievement. Their evidence that noncognitive skills matter rests on their interpretation of the error term in statistical analysis, rather than the empirical identification of specific skills, traits, or behaviors that contribute to wage differences.

Clearly identifying and measuring specific noncognitive factors becomes particularly important when we try to understand why there are differences in educational attainment by race/ethnicity, gender, or income. Knowing what to do to reduce these gaps requires knowing the extent to which they reflect underlying differences between groups in specific noncognitive skills, beliefs, behaviors, or strategies, or whether attainment differences are better explained by other factors entirely. Without identifying or measuring what these important noncognitive factors are, research does little to help practitioners or policymakers take action to impact differences in students' noncognitive factors as it is not clear what they need to address.

It is also possible that practitioners might develop strategies that are ineffective or even counterproductive if researchers do not make clear distinctions between evidence on noncognitive factors and inference about

them. For example, a much-cited study by Brian Jacob (2002) found that students' grades in middle school predict a large proportion of the gender gap in college enrollment and attributed differences in grades to noncognitive factors, reasoning that "conditional on cognitive ability, [grades are] determined by a variety of non-cognitive skills such as the ability to follow directions, work in groups, pay attention in class, and organize materials" (p. 591). The study did not actually measure students' ability to follow directions, work in groups, pay attention, or organize materials, and provided no evidence that there are gender differences in these behaviors. (It did measure time spent on homework and found that girls spent slightly more time per week than boys.) Yet practitioners might conclude from Jacob's assertion that they should invest time in further developing boys' academic behaviors. In fact, there are many different potential explanations for why boys in the middle grades have lower GPAs than girls, explanations that should be investigated if the GPA gap is to be addressed. For example, teachers might discriminate against boys when grading work. Parents could give boys more freedom to do their homework alone while monitoring their daughters more closely. Ten years ago, the American Association of University Women (AAUW) attributed the same gender differences we observe today—girls get better grades; boys get higher test scores—to gender bias in testing. Each of these interpretations is plausible, and there is nothing wrong with interpretation and debate; for research to be relevant for practitioners, however, it is important to delineate what is actually known from what seems promising but needs further study.

3. The need for more research on the role of school and classroom context in students' development and demonstration of noncognitive factors. Throughout this review, we have noted the role of classroom context in shaping noncognitive factors. Ultimately the practical goal of research on noncognitive factors is to help individual students become stronger learners who earn higher grades. This might suggest that a primary strategy to improve students' grades would be to focus on developing noncognitive factors as characteristics of individuals—implying that the "fix" is at the individual level. However, the research evidence to date suggests that trying to change noncognitive factors at the individual level in isolation from context may not be effective in the long term. Our case studies of school transitions highlight the importance of context for the enactment of noncognitive factors. For example, the large rise in absences and decline in studying behaviors when students move into high school show that students who exhibit strong academic behaviors in one context might not do so in another. To what extent are noncognitive factors located within individuals in ways that are transferable across context, and to what extent are they dependent on context?

Intervention studies of academic mindsets suggest some long-term effects on student achievement. However, it is not clear if they are helping students perform better in a particular context or whether they have changed something fundamental about each student's academic identity that will transfer across contexts. For example, seventh-graders who benefit from a growth mindset intervention have been shown to improve their performance during seventh grade with lasting effects to eighth grade, but we do not know what will happen as these students move from middle grades to high school. Likewise, interventions that normalize difficulty in the first year of college or increase the sense of belonging of African American students on elite college campuses improves their college performance, but we do not know if these benefits transfer from college to the workplace. Teaching students learning strategies seems promising, but again there is little research on its effectiveness across school contexts. At this point, we do not know to what extent interventions that focus on individuals can have lasting impacts on their engagement in learning across contexts.

We also want to recognize the role of the larger school context in shaping student performance. Throughout this review, we have looked at evidence on the role of classroom context and the availability of classroom strategies, but we know that teachers do not work in isolation. School-wide initiatives and structures, as well as school culture and environment, play a role in shaping students' experiences and performance in the classroom (Bryk, Sebring, Allensworth, Luppescu, & Easton, 2009). Research is also needed on the role of school contexts in promoting positive academic mindsets and on the work of school leaders in providing supports and professional development for teachers to build their capacity to address noncognitive factors in the classroom. Whether the best approach to leveraging noncognitive factors to improve student performance is through changing school and classroom contexts to be more supportive of students as learners or through targeting interventions at the individual level to address individual challenges depends in large part on the transferability of effects across contexts.

Designing future studies to address longitudinal questions will be very important for research going forward.

4. Teachers need coherent, actionable strategies for developing students as learners in the context of regular classroom instruction. If researchers strive for conceptual clarity and precise identification and measurement of individual noncognitive factors, this will help illuminate the mechanisms whereby each individual factor interacts with the others to affect student performance. However, where researchers need to pull everything apart and understand how it works, teachers need a coherent, integrated approach to build academic mindsets, learning strategies, social skills, academic behaviors, and academic perseverance as part of their everyday classroom practice. We cannot expect a teacher to implement separate interventions for all of the noncognitive factors that matter for their students' performance. Instead, they need guidance about how best to build classroom contexts and utilize pedagogical strategies that will leverage the body of research on noncognitive factors as they teach content and skills.

This is not to say that teachers are not an important audience for the research on noncognitive factors or that teaching as a profession does not need to take this research into account. But teachers should not be expected to focus on noncognitive factors as "another thing" to teach in isolation from the development of content knowledge and core academic skills. Fortunately, research from the learning sciences shows the tight interconnection between cognitive and noncognitive factors in shaping student learning and academic performance. For example, the evidence suggests that positive academic mindsets and learning strategies are developed through supporting students in engaging in challenging work. Teachers can design their classrooms so that they build mindsets, skills, behaviors, and strategies in pursuit of handling challenging content knowledge and developing core academic skills. Studies that seek to illuminate how this is all best pulled together in actual classrooms will provide an important step in bridging research and practice.

To the extent that we already have some knowledge base about how to develop positive mindsets and which learning strategies produce high learning gains, this knowledge needs to be much more accessible to teachers. Currently the vast majority of research on noncognitive factors is not written for a practitioner audience, and the literature is not available in places teachers are likely to go for professional learning. Bridging the gap between existing researcher knowledge and teacher practice is another important step.

There is also diffuse knowledge among practitioners that could inform practice broadly if it were systematically collected and disseminated. The most successful teachers may already have developed strategies that leverage noncognitive factors to engage students in learning. Researchers could gather evidence from practice to broaden our knowledge about how to do this. Such studies would need to be designed both to address unanswered questions and to incorporate what we already know. For example, we have strong evidence that noncognitive factors need to be understood along a developmental continuum. Separate studies of techniques and strategies used by effective instructors at the middle school, high school, and college levels would be helpful. Researchers should also consider gathering student-level data on mindsets, behaviors, skills, and strategies; any changes in these noncognitive factors should be measured over time for students in a given classroom as part of any study of effective classroom practices. In short, both empirical evidence and practice wisdom

exists that could contribute to a broader understanding of the role and development of noncognitive factors in academic achievement, but this evidence and wisdom is too often isolated by disciplinary boundaries as well as the gulf between research and practice. Collectively, we still know too little about how teachers and school leaders can incorporate attention to noncognitive factors into the everyday work of schools and classrooms. Future research should aim to bridge this divide.

The Promise of Noncognitive Factors in Teaching Adolescents To Become Learners

As this review indicates, we know much about the role of noncognitive factors in academic performance. But there is still much to be learned about how to leverage noncognitive factors to transform educational practice from its current focus on content knowledge and testable academic skills to the broader development of adolescents as learners. Decades of research inform our understanding and point us towards promising practices in the classroom. Our conceptual framework organizes different categories of noncognitive factors and models how they fit together to affect student performance. This provides a foundation for future research and a framework for practice. Teaching adolescents to become learners requires more than improving test scores; it means transforming classrooms into places alive with ideas that engage students' natural curiosity and desire to learn in preparation for college, career, and meaningful adult lives. This requires schools to build not only students' skills and knowledge but also their sense of what is possible for themselves, as they develop the strategies, behaviors, and attitudes that allow them to bring their aspirations to fruition.

TABLE 9.1

Summary of Evidence on Noncognitive Factors

Relationship to Academic Performance	
Academic Behaviors	All aspects of academic performance, cognitive and noncognitive, are expressed through academic behaviors. They have both a strong direct and indirect effect on grades.
Academic Perseverance	Research often conflates students' innate tendency to be perseverant with the actual behavior of doing work. While academic perseverance shows moderate relationships to student performance in cross-sectional designs, longitudinal studies find more modest relationships, making it difficult to establish evidence of a causal relationship between perseverance and performance.
Academic Mindsets	The effects of various school-based interventions suggest not only that mindsets are important but also that changing students' mindsets can result in improvements in academic performance.
Learning Strategies	Despite limitations, research shows that knowing how and when to use learning strategies is associated with higher overall learning and better academic success
Social Skills	Weakest evidence of direct relationship to grades.
	Much of the work done in the area of social skills training programs focuses on younger children, and there is only an indirect link between social skills and academic performance.
	A serious limitation of the studies showing a link between social skills and academic achievement is that almost all are correlational rather than causal. Studies tend to confound social skills with other variables, making it difficult to isolate the effect of social skills on academic performance.

Malleable	
Academic Behaviors	All types of human behavior are considered to be possible to change.
Academic Perseverance	The malleability of academic perseverance depends on how one defines perseverance. Evidence suggests that grit is fairly stable as an individual trait. However, students are more likely to display academic perseverance when they have positive academic mindsets or strategies to successfully manage tasks.
Academic Mindsets	The apparent success of many of the mindsets interventions suggests that mindsets are malleable, that is, they can be changed intentionally.
Learning Strategies	Research strongly supports the idea that learning strategies are malleable and can be directly taught. But many of the studies reviewed measured strategy use and performance concurrently. While these studies showed strong relationships between the two, they left open the question of whether learning strategies can be effectively taught, and if so, if teaching such strategies would result in improved performance.
Social Skills	Research on social skills training programs has found that they are generally effective, although the methodological strengths of these studies vary.

TABLE 9.1 *CONTINUED*

Summary of Evidence on Noncognitive Factors

Role of Classroom Context	
Academic Behaviors	Clear evidence that classroom context matters. Context shapes academic behaviors indirectly through its effect on other noncognitive factors, as well as directly through behavioral expectations and strategies.
Academic Perseverance	Classroom contexts that are structured to support students' success at assigned tasks and that provide students with strategies to make the tasks easier, make it more likely for students to persevere at those tasks.
Academic Mindsets	There is a theoretical and empirical basis for the importance of context in shaping mindsets. The effect of classrooms on student mindsets is particularly salient for racial/ethnic minority students.
Learning Strategies	Classrooms are important both as sites for the explicit teaching of subject-specific learning strategies and as contexts that set motivational conditions for learning strategy use.
Social Skills	Schools and classrooms play an important role in shaping students' social behaviors. Student behaviors are responsive to interpersonal, instructional, and environmental factors in the classroom.

Clear Strategies	
Academic Behaviors	While there are a wide range of classroom-based and school-wide strategies, few strategies have been evaluated on large scale basis. Academic behaviors such as attendance and assignment completion can be affected by close monitoring and support. Whole school reform shows some effects, but it is unclear what is responsible for changing behavior.
Academic Perseverance	There are numerous instructional practices which have been shown to improve students' perseverance in their coursework by changing students' mindsets. There is little research on whether and how teachers might structure classes to develop students' perseverance in the long run.
Academic Mindsets	There are a variety of short-term interventions that have evidence of success—from programs focused on envisioning "future possible selves" to "developing a sense of belonging." But while each individual study points to a relationship between mindsets and school performance, educational attainment, or other life-course outcomes, the broad array of findings across studies is confusing, and the directions for practice are unclear. There are few resources available currently that would translate social-psychological theory into classroom-based instructional practices that could be readily employed by teachers in a variety of school settings.
Learning Strategies	There are numerous short-term studies that provide evidence for the effectiveness of the teaching of specific strategies. Teacher feedback can provide ongoing formal and informal assessments so students can understand which strategies worked for them and where they need to improve. Student self-assessments can also provide opportunity for students to critique their strategies. Students can talk about their thinking with their teachers when planning out an academic task.
Social Skills	There is little direction for classroom teachers wanting to support the positive development of social skills in their students outside of a formal program.

79

TABLE 9.1 *CONTINUED*

Summary of Evidence on Noncognitive Factors

Would Changing This Factor Narrow the Achievement Gap?	
Academic Behaviors	There is evidence that academic behaviors explain part, but not all, of the gender gap in grades. There is little consistent evidence that academic behaviors explain differences in grades by race/ethnicity, particularly when controlling for test scores and economic status.
Academic Perseverance	Despite the fact that differences in perseverance by race or gender have been suggested as an explanation for race/ethnicity or gender differences in student academic performance, there is no research that has examined this directly.
Academic Mindsets	A number of interventions targeting mindsets have been shown to reduce gender and racial/ethnic achievement gaps. Ultimately, whether a focus on mindsets can narrow current gaps in performance and degree attainment depends on how much of the gap is caused by stereotype threat or other forces that differentially harm minority students in the first place.
Learning Strategies	Little evidence across studies about measured differences in learning strategies by race/ethnicity or gender.
Social Skills	Research gives little indication as to whether changes in students' social skills would narrow racial/ethnic and/or gender achievement gaps.

References

Ajzen, I. (2001)
Nature and operation of attitudes. *Annual Review of Psychology, 52*, 27-58.

Allensworth, E., Correa, M., and Ponisciak, S. (2008)
From high school to the future: ACT preparation—Too much, too late. Why ACT scores are low in Chicago and what it means for schools. Chicago: University of Chicago Consortium on Chicago School Research.

Allensworth, E., and Easton, J.Q. (2005)
The on-track indicator as a predictor of high school graduation. Chicago: University of Chicago Consortium on Chicago School Research.

Allensworth, E., and Easton, J.Q. (2007)
What matters for staying on-track and graduating in Chicago Public Schools. Chicago: University of Chicago Consortium on Chicago School Research.

Allensworth, E., and Luppescu, S. (2010)
Cross-classified random effects analysis of high school course grades and absences as value-added measures. Paper presented at the Meetings of the American Educational Research Association, Denver, CO.

Allensworth E., Gwynne, J., Sebastian, J., and Pareja, A. (2012)
The costs of increasing instructional rigor: Research series. Chicago: University of Chicago Consortium on Chicago School Research.

Ames, C. (1992)
Classrooms: Goals, structures, and student motivation. *Journal of Educational Psychology, 84*(3), 261-271.

Ames, C., and Archer, J. (1988)
Achievement goals in the classroom: Students' learning strategies and motivation processes. *Journal of Educational Psychology, 80*(3), 260-267.

Anderman, E.M., and Maehr, M.L. (1994)
Motivation and schooling in the middle grades. *Review of Educational Research, 64*(2), 287-309.

Anderson, E. (1999)
Code of the street: Decency, violence, and the moral life of the inner city. New York: W. W. Norton.

Aronson, J., Cohen, G., and McColskey, W. (2009)
Reducing stereotype threat in classrooms: A review of social-psychological intervention studies on improving the achievement of Black students. (Regional Education Laboratory, REL 2009-086) National Center for Education Evaluation and Regional Assistance, Institute for Education Science, U.S. Department of Education.

Aronson, J., Fried, C.B., and Good, C. (2002)
Reducing the effects of stereotype threat on African American college students by shaping theories of intelligence. *Journal of Experimental Social Psychology, 38*, 113-125.

Arum, R., and Roksa, J. (2011)
Academically adrift: Limited learning on college campuses. Chicago: University of Chicago Press.

Ashland School District. (2012)
Grading policy. Retrieved from http://www.ashland.k12.or.us/Page.asp?NavID=837.

Assessment Reform Group. (2002)
Testing, motivation, and learning. Cambridge, UK: University of Cambridge Faculty of Education.

Astin, A.W. (1993)
What matters in college? Four critical years revisited (1st ed.). San Francisco: Jossey-Bass.

Atkinson, J.W. (1957)
Motivational determinants of risk-taking behavior. *Psychological Review, 64*, 359-372.

Aud, S., Kewal Ramani, A., and Frohlich, L. (2011)
America's youth: Transitions to adulthood. Washington, DC: National Center for Education Statistics. Institute of Education Sciences, U.S. Department of Education.

Austin, S., and McCann, R. (1992, March)
Here's another arbitrary grade for your collection: A state-wide study of grading policies. Paper presented at the Annual Meeting of the American Educational Research Association, San Francisco, CA. (ERIC Document Reproduction Service No. 343 944).

Azevedo, R. (2005)
Using hypermedia as a metacognitive tool for enhancing student learning? The role of self-regulated learning. *Educational Psychologist, 40*(4), 199-209.

Balfanz, R., and Neild, R.C. (2006)
An extreme degree of difficulty: The educational demographics of urban neighborhood high schools. *Journal of Education for Students Placed at Risk, 11*(2): 123-141.

Bandura, A. (1977)
Social Learning Theory. Morristown, NJ: General Learning Press.

Bandura, A. (1978)
The self system in reciprocal determinism. *American Psychologist, 33*, 344-358.

Bandura, A. (1986)
Social foundations of thought and action: A social cognitive theory. Englewood Cliffs, NJ: Prentice Hall.

Bandura, A. (1997)
Self-efficacy: The exercise of control. New York: Freeman.

Bandura, A. (2001)
Social cognitive theory: An agentic perspective. *Annual Review of Psychology, 52,* 1-26.

Bandura, A., and Schunk, D.H. (1981)
Cultivating competence, self-efficacy, and intrinsic interest through proximal self-motivation. *Journal of Personality and Social Psychology, 41,* 586-598.

Barsalou, L.W. (2010)
Introduction to thirtieth anniversary perspectives on cognitive science: Past, present, and future. *Topics in Cognitive Science, 2,* 322-327.

Battistich, V., Solomon, D., Kim, D., Watson, M., and Schaps, E. (1995)
Schools as communities, poverty levels of student populations, and students' attitudes, motives, and performance: A multilevel analysis. *American Educational Research Journal, 32*(3), 627-658.

Bauer, L., Guerino, P., Noelle, K.L., and Tang, S. (2008)
Student victimization in U.S. schools: Results from the 2005 school crime supplement to the National Crime Victimization Survey (NCES 2009-306). Washington, DC: National Center for Education Statistics. Institute of Education Sciences, U.S. Department of Education.

Beelmann, A., Pfingsten, U., and Losel, F. (1994)
Effects of training social competence in children: A meta-analysis of recent evaluation studies. *Journal of Clinical Child Psychology, 23*(3), 260-271.

Bembenutty, H., and Karabenick, S.A. (1998)
Academic delay of gratification. Learning and individual differences, 10(4), 329-346.

Berger, P.L., and Luckmann, T. (1966)
The social construction of reality: A treatise in the sociology of knowledge. New York: Anchor.

Berger, J.B., and Milem, J.F. (1999)
The role of student involvement and perceptions of integration in a causal model of student persistence. *Research in Higher Education, 40*(6), 641-664.

Berliner, D.C. (1984)
The half-full glass: A review of research in teaching. In P.L. Hosford (Ed.), *Using what we know about teaching* (pp. 51-77). Alexandria, VA: Association for Supervision and Curriculum Development.

Bierman, K.L. (1986)
Process of change during social skills training with preadolescents and its relation to treatment outcome. *Child Development, 57,* 230-240.

Bierman, K.L., and Furman, W. (1984)
The effects of social skills training and peer involvement on the social adjustment of preadolescents. *Child Development, 55,* 151-162.

Bierman, K.L., Miller, C.L., and Stabb, S.D. (1987)
Improving the social behavior and peer acceptance of rejected boys: Effects of social skill training with instructions and prohibitions. *Journal of Consulting and Clinical Psychology, 55*(2), 194-200.

Bill & Melinda Gates Foundation. (2011)
Supporting students: Investing in innovation and quality. College-ready work monographs. Seattle, WA: Author. Retrieved January 21, 2012, from http://www.gates-foundation.org/highschools/Documents/supporting-students.pdf.

Black, P., and Wiliam, D. (2004)
The formative purpose: Assessment must first promote learning. In M. Wilson (Ed.), Toward coherence between classroom assessment and accountability. 103rd Yearbook of the National Society for the Study of Education (pp. 20-50). Chicago: University of Chicago Press.

Blackwell, L.S., Trzesniewski, K.H., and Dweck, C.S. (2007)
Implicit theories of intelligence predict achievement across an adolescent transition: A longitudinal study and an intervention. *Child Development, 78*(1), 246-263.

Blakey, E., and Spence, S. (1990)
Developing metacognition. (Report No. EDO-IR-90-6). Washington, DC: Office of Educational Research and Improvement (ERIC Document Reproduction Service No. ED327218).

Blanchfield, W.C. (1972)
College dropout identification: An economic analysis. *Journal of Human Resources, 7*(4), 540-544.

Blum, R.W., and Libbey, H.P. (2004)
School connectedness: Strengthening health and education outcomes for teenagers. *Journal of School Health, 74,* 229-299.

Blyth, D.A., Simmons, R.G., and Carlton-Ford, S. (1983)
The adjustment of early adolescents to school transitions. *Journal of Early Adolescence, 3,* 105-120.

Boekaerts, M., Zeidner, M., and Pintrich, P.R. (Eds.). (2000)
Handbook of self-regulation. San Diego, CA: Elsevier, Academic Press.

Bond, L.A., and Hauf, A.M.C. (2004)
Taking stock and putting stock in primary prevention: Characteristics of effective programs. *Journal of Primary Prevention, 24,* 199-221.

Borghans, L., Duckworth, A.L., Heckman, J.J., and ter Weel, B. (2008)
The economics and psychology of personality traits. *Journal of Human Resources, 43* (4), 972-1059.

Bouffard-Bouchard, T. (1990)
Influence of self-efficacy on performance in a cognitive task. *Journal of Social Psychology, 130*, 353-363.

Bowen, W.G., Chingos, M.M., and McPherson, M.S. (2009)
Crossing the finish line: Completing college at America's public universities. Princeton, NJ: Princeton University Press.

Bowles, S., and Gintis, H. (1976)
Schooling in capitalist America. New York: Basic Books.

Boyle, D.J., and Hassett-Walker, C. (2008)
Reducing overt and relational aggression among young children: The results from a two-year outcome evaluation. *Journal of School Violence, 7*(1), 27-42.

Bozick, R.N., and Dempsey, T.L. (2010)
Effort. In J.A. Rosen, E.J. Glennie, B.W. Dalton, J.M. Lennon, and R.N. Bozick (Eds.), *Noncognitive skills in the classroom: New perspectives on educational research* (pp. 39-68). Research Triangle Park, NC: RTI International.

Bradford, C., Muraskin, L, Cahalan, M., and Rak, R. (1997)
National study of student support services. Third-year longitudinal study results and program implementation study update. Washington, DC: Department of Education.

Bradshaw, C., Reinke, W., Brown, L., Bevans, K., and Leaf, P. (2008)
Implementation of school-wide positive behavioral interventions and supports (PBIS) in elementary schools: Observations from a randomized trial. *Education and Treatment of Children, 31*, 1-26.

Bransford, J.D., Brown, A.L., and Cocking, R.R. (2000)
How people learn: Brain, mind, experience, and school. Washington, DC: National Academy Press.

Brantlinger, E. (1991)
Social class distinctions in adolescents' reports of problems and punishment in school. *Behavioral Disorders, 17*, 36-46.

Braunstein, A., McGrath, M., and Pescatrice, D. (2000)
Measuring the impact of financial factors on college persistence. *Journal of College Student Retention: Research, Theory & Practice, 2*(3), 191-204.

Bridgeland, J.M., DiJulio, J.J., Jr., and Morison, K.B. (2006, March)
The silent epidemic: Perspectives of high school dropouts. Washington, DC: Civic Enterprises.

Brookhart, S.M. (1994)
Teachers' grading: Practices and theory. *Applied Measurement in Education, 7*(4), 279-301.

Brookhart, S.M. (2004)
Grading. Upper Saddle River, NJ: Pearson.

Brophy, J.E. (1981)
Teacher praise: A functional analysis. *Review of Educational Research, 51*, 5-32.

Bruner, J.S. (1960)
The process of education. Cambridge: Harvard University Press.

Bryk, A.S., and Driscoll, M.E. (1988)
The high school as community: Contextual influences and consequences for students and teachers. Madison, WI: National Center on Effective Secondary Schools.

Bryk, A.S., Sebring, P.B., Allensworth, E., Luppescu, S., and Easton, J.Q. (2009)
Organizing schools for improvement: Lessons from Chicago. Chicago: University of Chicago Press.

Butler, D.L., and Winne, P.H. (1995)
Feedback and self-regulated learning: A theoretical synthesis. *Review of Educational Research, 65*, 245-281.

Butler, R., and Nisan, M. (1986)
Effects of no feedback, task-related comments, and grades on intrinsic motivation and performance. *Journal of Educational Psychology, 78*(3), 210-216.

Button, S.B., Mathieu, J.E., and Zajac, D.M. (1996)
Goal orientation in organizational research: A conceptual and empirical foundation. *Organizational Behavior and Human Decision Processes, 67*(1), 26-48.

Cabrera, A.F., Nora, A., and Castaneda, M.B. (1992)
The role of finances in the persistence process: A structural model. *Research in Higher Education, 33*(5), 571-591.

Camara, W.J. (1998, May)
High school grading policies. College Board Research Notes, RN-04, 1-4.

Camara, W.J., and Echternacht, G. (2000, July)
The SAT I and high school grades: Utility in predicting success in college. The College Board Research Notes, RN-10, 1-12.

Camara, W.J., Kimmel, E., Scheuneman, J., and Sawtell, E.A. (2003)
Whose grades are inflated? College Board Research Report No. 2003-4. New York: College Board.

Camara, W.J., and Michaelides, M. (2001, March)
AP use in admissions: A response to Geiser and Santelices. New York: College Board.

Caprara, G.V., Vecchione, M., Alessandri, G., Gerbino, M., and Barbaranelli, C. (2011)
The contribution of personality traits and self-efficacy beliefs to academic achievement: A longitudinal study. *British Journal of Educational Psychology, 81*(1), 78-96.

Carr, P., and Walton, G.M. (2011)
Working harder together: A sense of working with others increases intrinsic motivation. *Manuscript submitted for publication.*

Carter, P. (2003)
"Black" cultural capital, status positioning, and schooling conflicts for low-income African American youth. *Social Problems, 50*(1), 136-155.

83

Casner-Lotto, J., Barrington, L., and Wright, M. (2006)
Are they really ready to work? Employers' perspectives on the basic knowledge and applied skills of new entrants to the twenty-first century U.S. workforce. Report Number BED-06-WF-KF. New York: The Conference Board, Corporate Voices for Working Families, the Partnership for Twenty-first Century Skills, and the Society for Human Resource Management.

Catalano, R.F., Berglund, M.L., Ryan, J.A.M., Lonczak, H.S., and Hawkins, J.D. (2002)
Positive youth development in the United States: Research findings on evaluations of positive youth development programs. *Prevention & Treatment, 5*, Article 15. doi: 10.1037/1522-3736.5.1.515a.

Character Education Partnership. (2008, April)
Performance values: Why they matter and what schools can do to foster their development. Position Paper. Washington, DC: Author. Retrieved January 21, 2012, from http://www.drake.edu/icd/PDFs/Performance_Values.pdf.

Clarke, M., Shore, A., Rhoades, K., Abrams, L.M., Miao, J., and Li, J. (2003)
Perceived effects of state-mandated testing programs on teaching and learning: Findings from interviews with educators in low-, medium-, and high-stakes states. Boston: National Board on Educational Testing and Public Policy, Lynch School of Education, Boston College.

cognitive. (n.d.). Merriam-Webster's Medical Dictionary
Retrieved June 23, 2011, from http://dictionary.reference.com/browse/cognitive.

Cohen, G.L., and Garcia, J. (2008)
Identity, belonging, and achievement: A model, interventions, implications. *Current Directions in Psychological Science, 17*(6), 365-369.

Cohen, G.L., Garcia, J., Apfel, N., and Master, A. (2006)
Reducing the racial achievement gap: A social-psychological intervention. *Science, 313*, 1307–1310.

Cohen, G.L., Garcia, J., Purdie-Vaughns, V., Apfel, N., and Brzustoski, P. (2009)
Recursive processes in self-affirmation: Intervening to close the minority achievement gap. *Science, 324*, 400-403.

Cohen, G.L., and Steele, C.M. (2002)
A barrier of mistrust: How negative stereotypes affect cross-race mentoring. In J. Aronson (Ed.), *Improving academic achievement: Impact of psychological factors on education* (pp. 303-327). San Diego, CA: Academic Press.

Cohen, G.L., Steele, C.M., and Ross, L.D. (1999)
The mentor's dilemma: Providing critical feedback across the racial divide. *Personality and Social Psychology Bulletin, 25*, 1302-1318.

Coie, J.D., and Krehbiel, G. (1984)
Effects of academic tutoring on the social status of low-achieving, socially rejected children. *Child Development, 55*, 1465-1478.

Coleman, M., Pfeiffer, S., and Oakland, T. (1992)
Aggression Replacement Training with behaviorally disordered adolescents. *Behavioral Disorders, 18*(1), 54-66.

Collaborative for Academic, Social, and Emotional Learning. (2003)
Safe and sound: An educational leader's guide to evidence-based social and emotional learning (SEL) programs. Chicago: Author. Retrieved February 12, 2012, from http://casel.org/publications/safe-and-sound-an-educational-leaders-guide-to-evidence-based-sel-programs/.

Conard, M.A. (2006)
Aptitude is not enough: How personality and behavior predict academic performance. *Journal of Research in Personality, 40*, 339-346.

Conchas, G.Q. (2006)
The color of success: Race and high-achieving urban youth. New York: Teachers College Press.

Conley, D.T. (2003)
Understanding university success. Eugene, OR: Center for Educational Policy Research, University of Oregon.

Conley, D.T. (2005)
College knowledge: What it really takes for students to succeed and what we can do to get them ready. San Francisco: Jossey-Bass.

Conley, D. (2007)
Toward a more comprehensive conception of college readiness. Eugene OR: Educational Policy Improvement Center.

Cook, T.D., Habib, F., Phillips, M., Settersten, R.A., Shagle, S.C., and Degirmencioglu, S.M. (1999)
Comer's school development program in Prince George's County, Maryland: A theory-based evaluation. *American Educational Research Journal, 36*, 543-597.

Cooper, H. (1989)
Homework. New York: Longman.

Cooper, H., Robinson, J.C., and Patall, E.A. (2006)
Does homework improve academic achievement? A synthesis of research, 1987-2003. *Review of Educational Research, 76*(1), 1-62.

Cordova, D.I., and Lepper, M.R. (1996)
Intrinsic motivation and the process of learning: Beneficial effects of contextualization, personalization, and choice. *Journal of Educational Psychology, 88*, 715-730.

Covington, M.V. (1984)
The self-worth theory of achievement motivation: Findings and implications. *The Elementary School Journal, 85*(1), 4-20.

Covington, M.V. (2000)
Goal theory, motivation, and school achievement: An integrative review. *Annual Review of Psychology, 51*, 171-200.

Covington, M.V., and Müeller, K.J. (2001)
Intrinsic versus extrinsic motivation: An approach/ avoidance reformulation. *Educational Psychology Review, 13*, 157-176.

Cragg, K. (2009)
Influencing the probability for graduation at four-year institutions: A multi-model analysis. *Research in Higher Education, 50*(4), 394-413.

Credé, M., and Kuncel, N.R. (2008)
Study habits, skills, and attitudes: The third pillar supporting collegiate academic performance. *Perspectives on Psychological Science, 3*, 425-453.

Crick, N.R., and Dodge, K.A. (1994)
A review and reformulation of social information-processing mechanisms in children's social adjustment. *Psychological Bulletin, 115*, 74-101.

Crocker, J., Voelkl, K., Testa, M., and Major, B. (1991)
Social stigma: The affective consequences of attributional ambiguity. *Journal of Personality & Social Psychology, 60*, 218-228.

Crockett, L.J., Petersen, A., Graber, J., Schulenberg, J.E., and Ebata, A. (1989)
School transitions and adjustment during early adolescence. *Journal of Early Adolescence, 9*, 181-210.

Crooks, T.J. (1988)
The impact of classroom evaluation practices on students. *Review of Educational Research, 58*, 438-481.

Cross, L.H., and Frary, R.B. (1999)
Hodgepodge grading: Endorsed by students and teachers alike. *Applied Measurement in Education, 12*(1), 53-72.

Cunha, F., Heckman, J.J., Lochner, L.J., and Masterov, D.V. (2006)
Interpreting the evidence on life cycle skill formation. In E.A. Hanushek and F. Welch (Eds.), *Handbook of the economics of education* (pp. 697-812). Amsterdam: North-Holland.

Cury, F., Elliot, A.J., Da Fonseca, D., and Moller, A.C. (2006)
The social-cognitive model of achievement motivation and the 2×2 achievement goal framework. *Journal of Personality and Social Psychology, 90*, 666-679.

Dallas Independent School District. (2008)
PK-12 Guidelines for grading. Retrieved March 26, 2012, from http://www.dallasisd.org/cms/lib/TX01001475/ Centricity/Domain/12/gradingguidelines.pdf.

Dalton, B.W. (2010)
Antisocial and prosocial behavior. In J.A. Rosen, E.J. Glennie, B.W. Dalton, J.M. Lennon, and R.N. Bozick (Eds.), *Noncognitive skills in the classroom: New perspectives on educational research* (pp. 145-168). Research Triangle Park, NC: RTI International.

Damon, W. (2008)
The path to purpose: Helping our children find their calling in life. New York: The Free Press.

Darling-Hammond, L., and Rustique-Forrester, E. (2005)
The consequences of student testing for teaching and teacher quality. *Yearbook of the National Society for the Study of Education, 104*(2), 289-319.

Deci, E.L. (1992)
The relation of interest to the motivation of behavior: A self-determination theory perspective. In K.A. Renninger, S. Hidi, and A. Kapp (Eds.), *The role of interest in learning and development* (pp. 43-70). Hillsdale, NJ: Erlbaum.

Deci, E.L., and Ryan, R.M. (1985)
Intrinsic motivation and self-determination in human behavior. New York: Plenum Press.

Delpit, L. (2006)
Other people's children: Cultural conflict in the classroom. New York: The New Press.

DesJardins, S.L., Ahlburg, D.A., and McCall, B.P. (1999)
An event history model of student departure. *Economics of Education Review, 18*(3), 375-390.

Dewey, J. (1958)
Experience and education. New York: Macmillan.

Dignath, C., Büttner, G., and Langfeldt, H.P. (2008)
How can primary school students learn self-regulated learning strategies most effectively? A meta-analysis on self-regulation training programmes. *Educational Research Review, 3*(2), 101-129.

Dill, E., and Boykin, A.W. (2000)
The comparative influence of individual, peer tutoring, and communal learning on the text recall of African American children. *Journal of Black Psychology, 26*, 65-78.

Dinsmore, D.L., Alexander, P.A., and Loughlin, S.M. (2008)
Focusing the conceptual lens on metacognition, self-regulation, and self-regulated learning. *Education Psychological Review, 20*, 391-409.

DiPerna, J.C., and Elliott, S.N. (1999)
The development and validation of the Academic Competence Evaluation Scales. *Journal of Psychoeducational Assessment, 17*, 207-225.

Duckworth, A.L. (2009)
True grit: Can perseverance be taught? [video file] Ted Talks. Retrieved January 27, 2012, from http://www.youtube.com/watch?v=qaeFnxSfSC4.

Duckworth, A.L., Grant, H., Loew, B., Oettingen, G., and Gollwitzer, P.M. (2011)
Self-regulation strategies improve self-discipline in adolescents: Benefits of mental contrasting and implementation intentions. *Educational Psychology, 31*(1), 17-26.

Duckworth, A.L., Peterson, C., Matthews, M.D., and Kelly, D.R. (2007)
Grit: Perseverance and passion for long-term goals. *Journal of Personality and Social Psychology, 92*, 1087-1101.

Duckworth, A.L., and Quinn, P.D. (2009)
Development and validation of the short grit scale (grit-s). *Journal of Personality Assessment, 91*, 166-174.

Duckworth, A.L., and Seligman, M.E.P. (2005)
Self-discipline outdoes IQ in predicting academic perfor-mance of adolescents. *Psychological Science, 16,* 939-44.

Duckworth, A.L., and Seligman, M.E.P. (2006)
Self-discipline gives girls the edge: Gender in self-discipline, grades, and achievement test scores. *Journal of Educational Psychology, 98*(1), 198-208.

Durlak, J.A. (1997)
Successful prevention programs for children and adolescents. New York: Plenum.

Durlak, J.A., Furhman, T., and Lampman, C. (1991)
Effectiveness of cognitive-behavior therapy for maladapting children: A meta-analysis. *Psychological Bulletin, 110*(2), 204-214.

Durlak, J.A., Weissberg, R.P., Dymnicki, A.B., Taylor, R.D., and Schellinger, K.B. (2011)
The impact of enhancing students' social and emotional learning: A meta-analysis of school-based universal inter-ventions. *Child Development, 82*(1), 405-432.

Dusenbury, L., and Falco, M. (1995)
Eleven components of effective drug abuse prevention curricula. *Journal of School Health, 65*(10), 420-425.

Dweck, C.S. (1975)
The role of expectations and attributions in the alleviation of learned helplessness. *Journal of Personality and Social Psychology, 31*(4), 674-685.

Dweck, C.S. (1986)
Motivational processes affecting learning. *American Psychologist, 41*(10), 1040-1048.

Dweck, C.S., and Leggett, E.L. (1988)
A social-cognitive approach to motivation and personality. *Psychological Review, 95,* 256-273.

Dweck, C.S., Walton, G.M., and Cohen, G.L. (2011)
Academic tenacity: Mindsets and skills that promote ong-term learning. White paper prepared for the Gates Foundation. Seattle, WA.

Eccles J.S., Adler, T.F., Futterman, R., Goff, S.B., Kaczala, C.M., Meece, J.L., and Midgley, C. (1983)
Expectancies, values, and academic behaviors. In J.T. Spence (Ed.), *Achievement and achievement motivation* (pp. 75-146). San Francisco: W.H. Freeman.

Eccles, J.S., Lord, S., and Midgley, C. (1991)
What are we doing to early adolescents? The impact of educational contexts on early adolescents. *American Journal of Education, 99*(4), 521-542.

Eccles, J.S., and Midgley, C. (1989)
Stage/environment fit: Developmentally appropriate classrooms for early adolescents. In R.E. Ames and C. Ames (Eds.), *Research on motivation in education* (Vol. 3, pp. 139-186). San Diego, CA: Academic Press.

Eccles, J., Midgley, C., and Adler, T.F. (1984)
Grade-related changes in the school environment: Effects on achievement motivation. In J.G. Nicholls (Ed.), *The development of achievement motivation* (pp. 283-331). Greenwich, CT: JAI Press.

Eccles, J.S., and Wigfield, A. (1995)
In the mind of the actor: The structure of adolescents' achievement task values and expectancy-related beliefs. *Personality and Social Psychology Bulletin, 21*(3), 215-225.

Eccles, J.S., and Wigfield, A. (2002)
Motivational beliefs, values and goals. *Annual Review of Psychology, 53,* 109-132.

Eisen, M., Zellman, G.L., and Murray, D.M. (2003)
Evaluating the Lions-Quest "Skills for Adolescence" drug education program: Second-year behavior outcomes. *Addictive Behaviors, 28,* 883-897.

Elliot, A.J., McGregor, H.A., and Gable, S. (1999)
Achievement goals, study strategies, and exam performance: A meditational analysis. *Journal of Educational Psychology, 91*(3), 549-563.

Engle, J. (2007)
Postsecondary access and success for first-generation college students. *American Academic 3*(1), 25-48.

Ericsson, K.A., and Smith, J. (1991)
Toward a general theory of expertise: Prospects and limits. Cambridge, England: Cambridge University Press.

Eskew, R.K., and Faley, R.H. (1988)
Some determinants of student performance in the first college-level financial accounting course. *The Accounting Review, LXIII*(1), 137-147.

Farkas, G. (1996)
Human capital or cultural capital? Ethnicity and poverty groups in an urban school district. New York: Aldine de Gruyter.

Farkas, G. (2003)
Cognitive skills and noncognitive traits and behaviors in stratification processes. *Annual Review of Sociology, 29,* 541-562.

Farkas, G., Grobe, R., Sheehan, D., and Shuan, Y. (1990)
Cultural resources and school success: Gender, ethnicity, and poverty groups within an urban school district. *American Sociological Review, 55,* 127-142.

Farrington, C.A. (2008)
Making sense of Fs: How high schools shape students' interpretations of and responses to failure. Doctoral dissertation, University of Illinois at Chicago.

Feldlaufer, H., Midgley, C., and Eccles, J. (1988)
Student, teacher, and observer perceptions of the class-room environment before and after the transition to junior high school. *Journal of Early Adolescence, 8,* 133-156.

86

Felner, R.D., Ginter, M., and Primavera, J. (1982)
Primary prevention during school transitions: Social support and environmental structure. *American Journal of Community Psychology, 10*, 277-290.

Feshbach, N.D., and Feshbach, S. (1987)
Affective processes and academic achievement. *Child Development, 58*, 1335-1347.

Flavell, J.H. (1963)
Piaget's legacy. *Psychological Science, 7*(4), 200-203.

Flavell, J.H. (1979)
Metacognition and cognitive monitoring: A new area of cognitive developmental inquiry. *American Psychologist, 34*, 906-911.

Flores-González, N. (2002)
School kids/street kids: Identity development in Latino students. New York: Teachers College Press.

Ford, J.K., Smith, E.M., Weissbein, D.A., Gully, S.M., and Salas, E. (1998)
Relationships of goal orientation, metacognitive activity, and practice strategies with learning outcomes and transfer. *Journal of Applied Psychology, 83*(2), 218-233.

Frary, R.B., Cross, L.H., and Weber, L.J. (1993)
Testing and grading practices and opinions of secondary teachers of academic subjects: Implications for instruction in measurement. *Educational measurement: Issues and Practice, 12*(3), 23-30.

Fraser, M.W., Galinsky, M.J., Smokowski, P.R., Day, S.H., Terzian, M.A., Rose, R.A., and Guo, S. (2005)
Social information-processing skills training to promote social competence and prevent aggressive behavior in the third grades. *Journal of Consulting and Clinical Psychology, 73*(6), 1045-1055

Furrer, C., and Skinner, E. (2003)
Sense of relatedness as a factor in children's academic engagement and performance. *Journal of Educational Psychology, 95*, 148-162.

Galassi, J.P., Gulledge, S.A., and Cox, N.D. (1997)
Middle school advisories: Retrospect and prospect. *Review of Educational Research, 67*(3), 301-338.

Gansemer-Topf, A., and Schuh, J. (2006)
Institutional selectivity and institutional expenditures: Examining organizational factors that contribute to retention and graduation. *Research in Higher Education, 47*(6), 613-642.

Garcia, J., and Cohen, G.L. (in press)
Social psychology and educational intervention. In E. Shafir (Ed.), *Behavioral foundations of policy.* New York, NY: Russell Sage.

Geiser, S., and Santelices, M.V. (2007)
Validity of high-school grades in predicting student success beyond the freshman year: High-school record versus standardized tests as indicators or four-year college outcomes. Research & Occasional Paper Series: CSHE.6.07. Berkeley: Center for Studies in Higher Education. Retrieved September 9, 2011, from http://cshe.berkeley.edu/publications/publications.php?id=265.

George, C. (2011, July 19)
Teaching secrets: Teaching students how to learn. *Education Week Teacher.* TLN, Teacher Leaders Network.

Glennie, E.J. (2010)
Coping and resilience. In J.A. Rosen, E.J. Glennie, B.W. Dalton, J.M. Lennon, and R.N. Bozick (Eds.), *Noncognitive skills in the classroom: New perspectives on educational research* (pp. 169-194). Research Triangle Park, NC: RTI International.

Good, C., Aronson, J., and Inzlicht, M. (2003)
Improving adolescents' standardized test performance: An intervention to reduce the effects of stereotype threat. *Journal of Applied Developmental Psychology, 24*, 645-662.

Goodenow, C. (1992)
Strengthening the links between educational psychology and the study of social contexts. *Educational Psychologist, 27*, 177-196.

Goodenow, C. (1993a)
Classroom belonging among early adolescent students: Relationships to motivation and achievement. *Journal of Early Adolescence, 13*(1), 21-43.

Goodenow, C. (1993b)
The psychological sense of school membership among adolescents: Scale development and educational correlates. *Psychology in the Schools, 30*(January), 79-90.

Goodenow, C., and Grady, K.E. (1993)
The relationship of school belonging and friends' values to academic motivation among urban adolescent students. *Journal of Experimental Education, 2*(1), 60-71.

Gordon, E.W., and Bridglall, B.L. (Eds.). (2006)
Affirmative development: Cultivating academic ability. Critical Issues in Contemporary American Education Series. Blue Ridge Summit, PA: Rowman & Littlefield.

Gore, P.A., Leuwerke, W.C., and Metz, A.J. (2009)
Noncognitive and motivational factors in student success. Retrieved February 12, 2012, from http://student strengthsinventory.com/Files/Noncognitive%20 Report.pdf.

Graham, S., and Harris, K. (1994)
The role and development of self-regulation in the writing process. In D.H. Schunk and B.J. Zimmerman (Eds.), *Self-regulation of learning and performance: Issues and educational applications* (pp. 209-228). Hillsdale, NJ: Erlbaum.

87

Grant, H., and Dweck, C.S. (2003)
Clarifying achievement goals and their impact. *Journal of Personality and Social Psychology, 85*(3), 541-553.

Green, K.D., Forehand, R., Beck, S.J., and Vosk, B. (1980)
An assessment of the relationships among measures of children's social competence and children's academic achievement. *Child Development, 51*, 1149-1156.

Greenberg, M.T., Weissberg, R.P., O'Brien, M.U., Zins, J.E., Fredericks, L., Resnik, H., and Elias, M.J. (2003, June/July)
Enhancing school-based prevention and youth development through coordinated social, emotional, and academic learning. *American Psychologist, 58*(6-7), 466-474.

Gregory, A., Skiba, R.J., and Noguera, P.A. (2010)
The achievement gap and the discipline gap: Two sides of the same coin? *Educational Researcher, 39*(1), 59-68.

Gresham, F.M. (1995)
Best practices in social skills training. In A. Thomas and J. Grimes (Eds.), *Best practices in school psychology-III* (pp. 1021-1030). Washington, DC: National Association of School Psychologists.

Gresham, F.M., and Elliott, S.N. (1990)
The social skills rating system. Circle Pines, MN: American Guidance Service.

Hacker, D.J., Bol, L., Horgan, D.D., and Rakow, E.A. (2000)
Test prediction and performance in a classroom context. *Journal of Educational Psychology, 92*, 160-170.

Hacker, D.J., Dunlosky, J., and Graesser, A.C. (Eds.). (2009)
Handbook of metacognition in education. New York: Routledge.

Hackett, G. (1985)
The role of mathematics self-efficacy in the choice of math-related majors of college women and men: A path analysis. *Journal of Counseling Psychology, 32*, 47-56.

Hackett, G., and Betz, N.E. (1989)
An exploration of the mathematics self-efficacy/mathematics performance correspondence. *Journal for Research in Mathematics Education, 20*, 261-273.

Hadwin, A.F., Nesbit, J.C., Jamieson-Noel, D., Code, J., and Winne, P.H. (2007)
Examining trace data to explore self-regulated learning. *Metacognition and Learning, 2*, 107-124.

Hagborg, W.J. (1992)
Grades and motivational orientation among high school students. *Journal of Psychoeducational Assessment, 10*, 355-361.

Hall, B.W., and Bacon, T.P. (2005)
Building a foundation against violence: Impact of a school-based prevention program on elementary students. *Journal of School Violence, 4*(4), 63–83.

Haller, E.P., Child, D.A., and Walberg, H.J. (1988)
Can comprehension be taught? A quantitative synthesis of "metacognitive" studies. *Educational Researcher, 17*(9), 5-8.

Hamre, B.K., and Pianta, R.C. (2005)
Can instructional and emotional support in the first-grade classroom make a difference for children at risk of school failure? *Child Development, 76*, 949-967.

Hamre, B.K., and Pianta, R.C. (2006)
Student-teacher relationships. In G.G. Bear and K.M. Minke (Eds.), *Children's needs III: Development, prevention, and intervention* (pp. 59-71). Bethesda, MD: National Association of School Psychologists.

Harber, K. (2004)
The positive feedback bias as a response to out-group unfriendliness. *Journal of Applied Social Psychology, 34*, 2272-2297.

Harter, S., Whitesell, N.R., and Kowalski, P. (1992)
Individual differences in the effects of educational transitions on young adolescents' perceptions of competence and motivational orientation. *American Educational Research Journal, 29*, 777-807.

Harvey, O.J. (Ed.). (1963)
Motivation and social interaction: Cognitive determinants. New York: Ronald Press.

Harvey, O.J., and Schroder, H.M. (1963)
Cognitive aspects of self and motivation. In O.J. Harvey (Ed.), *Motivation and social interaction-cognitive determinants.* (pp. 95-133). New York: Ronald Press.

Hattie, J., Biggs, J., and Purdie, N. (1996)
Effects of learning skills interventions on student learning. *Review of Educational Research, 66*(2), 99-136.

Hauser, R.M., and Palloni, A. (2011)
Adolescent IQ and survival in the Wisconsin longitudinal study. *The Journals of Gerontology, Series B: Psychological Sciences and Social Sciences, 66B*(S1), i91–i101, doi:10.1093/geronb/gbr037.

Hawkins, J.D., Catalano, R.F., Kosterman, R., Abbott, R., and Hill, K.G. (1999)
Preventing adolescent health-risk behaviors by strengthening protection during childhood. *Archives of Pediatrics & Adolescent Medicine, 153*(3), 226-234.

Hawkins, J.D., Guo, J., Hill, K.G., and Battin-Pearson, S. (2001)
Long-term effects of the Seattle Social Development Intervention on school bonding trajectories. *Applied Developmental Science, 5*(4), 225-236.

Hawkins, J.D., Smith, B.H., and Catalano, R.F. (2004)
Social development and social and emotional learning. In J.E. Zins, R.P. Weissberg, M.C. Wang, and H.J. Walberg (Eds.), *Building academic success on social and emotional learning: What does the research say?* (pp. 135-150). New York: Teachers College Press.

Heckman, J.J. (2008)
Schools, skills, and synapses. *Economic Inquiry, 46*(3), 289-324.

Heckman, J.J., and Rubinstein, Y. (2001)
The importance of noncognitive Skills: Lessons from the GED testing program. *American Economic Review, 91*(2), 145-149.

Helmke, A., and Schrader, F.W. (2001)
School achievement: Cognitive and motivational determinants. In N.J. Smelser and P.B. Baltes (Eds.). *International Encyclopedia of the Social & Behavioral Sciences* (pp. 13553-13554). New York: Elsevier Ltd.

Hoffman, J.L. (2002)
The impact of student cocurricular involvement on student success: Racial and religious differences. *The Journal of College Student Development, 43*(5), 712-739.

Hoffman, J.L., and Lowitzki, K.E. (2005)
Predicting college success with high school grades and test scores: Limitations for minority students. *The Review of Higher Education, 28*(4), 455-474.

Hu, S., and St. John, E.P. (2001)
Student persistence in a public higher education system: Understanding racial and ethnic differences. *Journal of Higher Education, 72*(3), 265-286.

Hulleman, C.S., and Harackiewicz, J.M. (2009)
Making education relevant: Increasing interest and performance in high school science classes. *Science, 326*, 1410-1412.

Hurtado, S., and Carter, D.F. (1997)
Effects of college transition and perceptions of the campus racial climate on Latino college students' sense of belonging. *Sociology of Education, 70*(4), 324-345.

Isaacson, R.M., and Fujita, F. (2006)
Metacognitive knowledge monitoring and self-regulated learning: Academic success and reflections on learning. *Journal of the Scholarship of Teaching and Learning, 6*(1), 39-55.

Izard, C.E. (2002)
Translating emotion theory and research into preventive interventions. *Psychological Bulletin, 128*, 796-824.

Jacob, B.A. (2002)
Where the boys aren't: Noncognitive skills, returns to school and the gender gap in higher education. *Economics of Education Review, 21*, 589-598.

Jennings, P.A., and Greenberg, M.T. (2009)
The prosocial classroom: Teacher social and emotional competence in relation to student and classroom outcomes. *Review of Educational Research, 79*, 491-525.

Johnson, D.W., and Johnson, R.T. (2009)
An educational psychology success story: Social interdependence theory and cooperative learning. *Educational Researcher, 3*(5), 365-379.

Johnson, D.W., Maruyama, G., Johnson, R., Nelson, D., and Skon, L. (1981)
The effects of cooperative, competitive, and individualistic goal structures on achievement: A meta-analysis. *Psychological Bulletin, 89*, 47-62.

Johnson, D.W., Stevens, W.D., Allensworth, E., de la Torre, M., Rosenkranz, T., and Pareja, A.S. (Forthcoming)
Free to Fail Research Series: Student-teacher relationships decline at a critical time. Chicago: University of Chicago Consortium on Chicago School Research

Kaestner, R. (2009, April)
Adolescent cognitive and noncognitive correlates of adult health. NBER Working Paper No. 14924. Cambridge, MA: National Bureau of Economic Research. Retrieved October 7, 2011, from http://www.nber.org/papers/w14924.

Kaplan, S., and Kaplan, R. (1982)
Cognition and environment: Functioning in an uncertain world. New York: Praeger.

Kaplan, D.S., Peck, B.M., and Kaplan, H.B. (1997)
Decomposing the academic failure-dropout relationship: A longitudinal analysis. *The Journal of Educational Research, 90*, 331-343.

Keith, T.Z. (1982)
Time spent on homework and high school grades: A large sample path analysis. *Journal of Educational Psychology, 74*(2), 248-253.

Keith, T.Z., and Benson, M.J. (1992)
Effects of manipulable influences on high school grades across five ethnic groups. *Journal of Educational Research, 86*, 85-93.

Keith, T.Z., and Cool, V.A. (1992)
Testing models of school learning: Effects of quality of instruction, motivation, academic coursework, and homework on academic achievement. *School Psychology Quarterly, 7*, 207-226.

Keith, T.Z., Diamond-Hallam, C., and Fine, J.G. (2004)
Longitudinal effects of in-school and out-of-school homework on high school grades. *School Psychology Quarterly, 19*(3), 187-211.

Keith, T.Z., Keith, P.B., Troutman, G.C., Bickley, P.G., Trivette, P.S., and Singh, K. (1993)
Does parental involvement affect eighth grade student achievement? Structural analysis of national data. *School Psychology Review, 22*, 472-494.

Kellaghan, T., Madaus, G., and Raczek, A. (1996)
The use of external examinations to improve student motivation. Washington, DC: American Educational Research Association.

Kelley, H.H. (1973)
The process of causal attribution. *American Psychologist, 28*, 107-128.

89

Kemple, J.J., and Herlihy, C.M. (2004)
Context, components, and initial impacts on ninth-grade students' engagement and performance: The Talent Development High School model. New York: MDRC.

Kemple, J.J., Herlihy, C.M., and Smith, T.J. (2005)
Making progress toward graduation: Evidence from the Talent Development High School Model. New York: MDRC.

Koretz, D. (2005)
Alignment, high stakes, and the inflation of test scores. *Yearbook of the National Society for the Study of Education, 104*(2), 99-118.

Kramarski, B., and Gutman, M. (2006)
How can self-regulated learning be supported in mathematical e-learning environments? *Journal of Computer Assisted Learning, 22*, 24-33.

Kramarski, B., and Zeichner, O. (2001)
Using technology to enhance mathematical reasoning: Effects of feedback and self-regulation learning. *Educational Media International, 38*(2-3), 77-82.

Kruck, S.E., and Lending, D. (2003)
Predicting academic performance in an introductory college-level IS course. *Information Technology, Learning, and Performance Journal, 21*(2), 9-15.

Kurlaender, M., Reardon, S.F., and Jackson, J. (2008)
Middle school predictors of high school achievement in three California school districts. California Dropout Research Project. Retrieved from http://www.cdrp.ucsb.edu/dropouts/pubs_reports.htm.

Kuther, T.L., and Fisher, C.B. (1998)
Victimization by community violence in young adolescents from a suburban city. *Journal of Early Adolescence, 18*, 53-76.

Ladd, G. (1981)
Effectiveness of social learning method for enhancing children's social interaction and peer acceptance. *Child Development, 12*, 171-178.

Ladd, G.W., and Mize, J. (1983)
A cognitive social learning model of social skill training. *Psychological Review, 90*, 127-157.

Lambert, N.M., and Nicholl, R.C. (1977)
Competence model of nonintellectual behavior and its relationship to early reading achievement. *Journal of Educational Psychology, 69*, 481-490.

Larson, K.A, and Rumberger, R.W. (1995)
ALAS: Achievement for Latinos through Academic Success. In H. Thornton (Ed.), *Staying in school: A technical report of the dropout prevention projects for junior high school students with learning and emotional disabilities.* Minneapolis, MN: University of Minnesota, Institute on Community Integration.

Le, H., Casillas, A., Robbins, S.B., and Langley, R. (2005)
Motivational and skills, social, and self-management predictors of college outcomes: Constructing the student readiness inventory. *Educational and Psychological Measurement, 65*(3), 482-508.

Lee, O., and Anderson, C.W. (1993)
Task engagement and conceptual change in middle school science classrooms. *American Educational Research Journal, 30*(3), 585-610.

Lee, D.L., and Axelrod, S. (2005)
Behavior modification: Basic principles. Austin, TX: Pro-Ed.

Lemerise, E.A., and Arsenio, W.F. (2000)
An integrated model of emotion processes and cognition in social information processing. *Child Development, 71*, 107-118.

Lennon, J.M. (2010)
Self-regulated learning. In J.A. Rosen, E.J. Glennie, B.W. Dalton, J.M. Lennon, and R.N. Bozick (Eds.), *Noncognitive skills in the classroom: New perspectives on educational research* (pp. 69-90). Research Triangle Park, NC: RTI International.

Lent, R.W., Brown, S.D., and Larkin, K.C. (1984)
Relation of self-efficacy expectations to academic achievement and persistence. *Journal of Counseling Psychology, 31*, 356-362.

Lent, R.W., Lopez, F.G., and Bieschke, K.J. (1991)
Mathematics self-efficacy: Sources and relation to science-based career choice. *Journal of Counseling Psychology, 38*, 424.

Li, G., and Killian, T. (1999)
Students who left college: An examination of their characteristics and reasons for leaving. *Paper presented at Association for Institutional Research*, Seattle, WA.

London, H.B. (1989)
Breaking away: A study of first-generation college students and their families. *American Journal of Education, 97*(2), 144-170.

Major, B., and Schmader, T. (1998)
Coping with stigma through psychological disengagement. In J.K. Swim and C. Stangor (Eds.), *Prejudice: The target's perspective* (pp. 219-241). San Diego, CA: Academic Press.

Malecki, C.K., and Elliott, S.N. (2002)
Children's social behaviors as predictors of academic achievement: A longitudinal analysis. *School Psychology Quarterly, 17*(1), 1-23.

Marzano, R.J. (2000)
Transforming classroom grading. Aurora, CO: Mid-continent Research for Education and Learning Institute.

Masten, A.S., and Coatsworth, J.D. (1998)
The development of competence in favorable and unfavorable environments: Lessons from research on successful children. *American Psychologist, 53*(2), 205-220.

McCarthy, J.D., and Hoge, D.R. (1987)
Social construction of school punishment. *Social Forces, 65*, 1101-1120.

McDonough, P., and Calderone, S. (2006)
The meaning of money: Perceptual differences between college counselors and low-income families about college costs and financial aid. *American Behavioral Scientist, 49*(12), 1703-1718.

McFadden, A.C., Marsh, G.E., Price, B.J, and Hwang, Y. (1992)
A study of race and gender bias in the punishment of handicapped school children. *Urban Review, 24*, 239-251.

McCombs, B.L. (1991)
Motivation and lifelong learning. *Educational Psychologist, 26*, 117-128.

McCombs, B.L. (1993)
Learner-centered psychological principles for enhancing education: applications in school settings. In L.A. Penner, G.M. Batsche, H.M. Knoff, and D.L. Nelson (Eds.), *The challenges in mathematics and science education: Psychology's response* (pp. 287-313). Washington, DC: American Psychological Association.

McCombs, B.L. (1994)
Strategies for assessing and enhancing motivation: Keys to promoting self-regulated learning and performance. In H.F. O'Neil, Jr., and M. Drillings (Eds.), *Motivation: Theory and research* (pp. 49-69). Hillsdale, NJ, England: Lawrence Erlbaum Associates, Inc.

McCrae, R.R., and Costa, P.T., Jr. (1994)
The stability of personality: Observations and evaluations. *Current Directions in Psychological Science, 3*, 173-175.

McGinnis, E., and Goldstein, A. (1997)
Skillstreaming the elementary school child: New strategies and perspectives for teaching prosocial skills. Champaign, IL: Research Press.

McKeachie, W.J., Pintrich, P.R., Lin, Y.G., and Smith, D. (1986)
Teaching and learning in the college classroom: A review of the research literature. Ann Arbor, MI: National Center for Research to Improve Postsecondary Teaching and Learning. The University of Michigan.

McKnight, P.E., and Kashdan, T.B. (2009)
Purpose in life as a system that creates and sustains health and well-being: An integrative, testable theory. *Review of General Psychology, 13*, 242-251.

McKoon, G., and Ratcliff, R. (1992)
Inference during reading. *Psychological Review, 99*, 440-466.

McMillan, D.W., and Chavis, D.M. (1986)
Sense of community: A definition and theory. *Journal of Community Psychology, 14*(January), 6-23.

Mendes, W.B., Major, B., McCoy, S., and Blascovich, J. (2008)
How attributional ambiguity shapes physiological and emotional response to social rejection and acceptance. *Journal of Personality and Social Psychology, 94*, 278-291.

Mendoza-Denton, R., Goldman-Flythe, M., Pietrzak, J., Downey, G., and Aceves, M.J. (2010)
Group-value ambiguity: Understanding the effects of academic feedback on minority students' self-esteem. *Social Psychological and Personality Science, 1*, 127-135.

Mendoza-Denton, R., Pietrzak, J., and Downey, G. (2008)
Distinguishing institutional identification from academic goal pursuit: Interactive effects of ethnic identification and race-based rejection sensitivity. *Journal of Personality and Social Psychology, 95*, 338-351.

metacognition. (n.d.). Dictionary.com's Twenty-first Century Lexicon.
Retrieved June 23, 2011, from http://dictionary.reference.com/browse/metacognition.

Mevarech, Z.R., and Kramarski, B. (1997)
IMPROVE: A multidimensional method for teaching mathematics in heterogeneous classrooms. *American Educational Research Journal 34*, 365-394.

Midgley, C., and Urdan, T. (2001)
Academic self-handicapping and achievement goals: A further examination. *Contemporary Educational Psychology, 26*(1), 61-75.

Miller, S.R. (1998)
Shortcut: High school grades as a signal of human capital. *Educational Evaluation and Policy Analysis, 20*, 299-311.

Miller, S.R., Allensworth, E., and Kochanek, J.R. (2002)
Student performance: Coursetaking, test scores, and outcomes. Chicago: University of Chicago Consortium on Chicago School Research.

Mischel, H.N., and Mischel, W. (1983)
The development of children's knowledge of self-controls trategies. *Child Development, 54*, 603-619.

Mischel, W., Shoda, Y., and Peake, P.K. (1988)
The nature of adolescent competencies predicted by preschool delay of gratification. *Journal of Personality and Social Psychology, 54*, 687-696.

Moffat, G.K. (1993, February)
The validity of the SAT as a predictor of grade point average for nontraditional college students. Paper presented at the annual meeting of the Eastern Educational Research Association, Clearwater Beach, FL. (ERIC Document Reproduction Service No. ED 356 252).

Mueller, C.M., and Dweck, C.S. (1998)
Intelligence praise can undermine motivation and performance. *Journal of Personality and Social Psychology, 75*, 33-52.

Munro, B.H. (1981)
Dropouts from higher education: Path analysis of a national sample. *American Educational Research Journal, 18*(2), 133-141.

Murnane, R.J., and Levy, F. (1996)
Teaching the new basic skills: Principles for educating children to thrive in a changing economy. New York: Free Press.

Nagda, B.A., Gregerman, S.R., Jonides, J., von Hippel, W., and Lerner, J.S. (1998)
Undergraduate student-faculty research partnerships affect student retention. *Review of Higher Education, 22*(1), 55-72.

National Research Council and the Institute of Medicine. (2004)
Engaging schools: Fostering high school students' motivation to learn. Washington, DC: National Academies Press.

Natriello, G., and McDill, E.L. (1986)
Performance standards, student effort on homework, and academic achievement. *Sociology of Education, 59*, 18-31.

Nava, F.J.G., and Loyd, B.H. (1992, April)
An investigation of achievement and nonachievement criteria in elementary and secondary school grading. Paper presented at the Annual Meeting of the American Educational Research Association, San Francisco, CA. (ERIC Document Reproduction Service No. ED 346 145).

Neild, R.C. (2009)
Falling off track during the transition to high school: What we know and what can be done. *The Future of Children, 19*, 53-76.

Neild, R.C., and Balfanz, R. (2001).
An extreme degree of difficulty: The educational demographics of the ninth grade in an urban school system. Paper presented at the annual meetings of the American Sociological Association, Anaheim, CA.

Neild, R.C., and Balfanz, R. (2006)
Unfulfilled promise: The causes and consequences of high school dropout in Philadelphia, 2000-2005. Philadelphia: The Philadelphia Youth Network.

Neild, R.C., Stoner-Eby, S., and Furstenberg, F. (2008)
Connecting entrance and departure: The transition to 9th grade and high school dropout. *Education and Urban Society, 40*(5), 543-569.

Neild, R., and Weiss, C. (1999)
The Philadelphia Education Longitudinal Study (PELS): Report on the transition to high school in the School District of Philadelphia. Philadelphia Education Fund: Philadelphia.

Nicholls, J.G. (1986)
Varieties of interpretation of achievement motivation: A reply to Kukla and Scher. *Psychological Review, 93*, 381-382.

Nicholls, J.G. (1989)
The competitive ethos and democratic education. Cambridge, MA: Harvard University Press.

Nicholls, J.G., and Miller, A.T. (1985)
Differentiation of the concept of luck and skill. *Developmental Psychology, 21*, 76-82.

Nora, A., Barlow, L., and Crisp, G. (2006)
Examining the tangible and psychological benefits of financial aid with student access, engagement, and degree attainment. *American Behavioral Scientist, 49*(12), 1636-1651.

Nota, L., Soresi, S., and Zimmerman, B.J. (2004)
Self-regulation and academic achievement and resilience: A longitudinal study. *International Journal of Educational Research, 41*(3), 198-215.

O'Connor, M.C., and Paunonen, S.V. (2007)
Big Five personality predictors of postsecondary academic performance. *Personality and Individual Differences, 43*, 971-990.

OECD. (2011)
Retrieved February 12, 2012, from www.oecd.org.

Oseguera, L., and Rhee, B.S. (2009)
The influence of institutional retention climates on student persistence to degree completion: A multilevel approach. *Research in Higher Education, 50*(6), 546-569.

Osterman, K.F. (2000)
Students' need for belonging in the school community. *Review of Educational Research, 70*(3), 323-367.

Oyserman, D., Bybee, D., and Terry, K. (2006)
Possible selves and academic outcomes: How and when possible selves impel action. *Journal of Personality and Social Psychology, 91*, 188-204.

Oyserman, D., and Fryberg, S. (2006)
The possible selves of diverse adolescents: Content and function across gender, race and national origin. In C. Dunkel and J. Kerpelman (Eds.), *Possible selves: Theory, research, and application* (pp. 17-39). New York: Nova Science.

Oyserman, D., and James, L. (2009)
Possible selves: From content to process. In K.D. Markman, W.M. Klein, and J.A. Suhr (Eds.), *The handbook of imagination and mental stimulation* (pp. 373-394). New York: Psychology Press.

Oyserman, D., Terry, K., and Bybee, D. (2002)
A possible selves intervention to enhance school involvement. *Journal of Adolescence, 25*, 313-326.

Page, B., and D'Agostino, A. (2005)
Connect with Kids: 2004-2005 Study results for Kansas and Missouri. Durham, NC: Compass Consulting Group.

Pajares, F. (1996)
Self-efficacy beliefs in academic settings.
Review of Educational Research, 66, 543-578.

Pajares, F., and Miller, M.D. (1994)
The role of self-efficacy and self-concept beliefs in mathematical problem-solving: A path analysis.
Journal of Educational Psychology, 86, 193-203.

Pajares, F., and Miller, M.D. (1995)
Mathematics self-efficacy and mathematics outcomes: The need for specificity of assessment.
Journal of Counseling Psychology, 42, 190-198.

Palincsar, A.S. (1986)
Metacognitive strategy instruction. *Exceptional Children, 53*(2), 118-124.

Paris, S.G., Lipson, M., and Wixson, K. (1983)
Becoming a strategic reader. *Contemporary Educational Psychology, 8,* 293-316.

Paris, S.G., Wasik, B., and Turner, J.C. (1996)
The development of strategic readers. In R. Barr, M.L. Kamil, P.B. Mosenthal, and P.D. Pearson (Eds.). *Handbook of reading research.* Vol. 2 (pp. 609-640). Hillsdale, NJ: Lawrence Erlbaum Associates, Inc.

Paris, S.G., and Winograd, P. (1990)
How metacognition can promote academic learning and instruction. In B.F. Jones and L. Idol (Eds.), *Dimensions of thinking and cognitive instruction* (pp. 15-51). Hillsdale, NJ: Lawrence Erlbaum Associates.

Pascarella, E., Terenzini, P., and Wolfle, L. (1986)
Orientation to college and freshman year persistence/withdrawal decisions. *Journal of Higher Education, 57*(2), 155-173.

Pelham, W.E., and Fabiano, G.A. (2008)
Evidence-based psychosocial treatment for attention deficit/hyperactivity disorder: An update. *Journal of Clinical Child and Adolescent Psychology, 37,* 185-214.

Peng S.S., and Wright, D. (1994)
Explanation of academic achievement of Asian American students. *Journal of Educational Research, 87,* 346-352.

Perry, T., Steele, C., and Hilliard, III, A. (2003)
Young, gifted, and Black: Promoting high achievement among African American students. Boston: Beacon Press.

Phelan, P., Davidson, A.L., and Cao, H.T. (1991)
Students' multiple worlds: Negotiating the boundaries of family, peer, and school cultures. *Anthropology & Education Quarterly, 22*(3), 224-250.

Picower, B. (2009)
The unexamined Whiteness of teaching: how White teachers maintain and enact dominant racial ideologies. *Race Ethnicity and Education, 12*(2), 197-215.

Pike, G.R., and Kuh, G.D. (2005)
First- and second-generation college students: A comparison of their engagement and intellectual development. *The Journal of Higher Education, 76*(3), 276-300.

Pintrich, P.R. (1989)
The dynamic interplay of student motivation and cognition in the college classroom. In C. Ames and M. Maehr (Eds.), *Advances in motivation and achievement: Motivation enhancing environments.* Vol. 6 (pp. 117-160). Greenwich, CT: JAI Press.

Pintrich, P.R. (2000)
Multiple goals, multiple pathways: The role of goal orientation in learning and achievement. *Journal of Educational Psychology, 92*(3), 544-555.

Pintrich, P.R., and De Groot, E. (1990)
Motivational and self-regulated learning components of classroom academic performance. *Journal of Educational Psychology, 82,* 33-40.

Pintrich, P.R., Smith, D.A.F., Garcia, T., and McKeachie, W.J. (1993)
Reliability and predictive validity of the Motivational Strategies for Learning Questionnaire (MSLQ). *Educational and Psychological Measurement, 53,* 801-813.

Pittsburgh Public Schools. (2009)
Memo regarding grading procedures. Retrieved March 26, 2012, from http://www.pps.k12.pa.us/143110127103415203/lib/143110127103415203/Updated_Committee_Grading_Memo.pdf.

Pokay, P., and Blumenfeld, P.C. (1990)
Predicting achievement early and late in the semester: The role of motivation and use of learning strategies. *Journal of Educational Psychology, 82,* 41-50.

Popham, W.J. (2000)
Modern educational measurement: Practical guidelines for educational leaders (3rd ed.). Boston: Allyn and Bacon.

Poropat, A.E. (2009)
A meta-analysis of the five-factor model of personality and academic performance. *Psychological Bulletin, 135*(2), 322-338.

Pressley, M., and Woloshyn, V. (Eds.). (1995)
Cognitive strategy instruction that really improves children's academic performance (2nd ed.). Cambridge, MA: Brookline Books.

Purdie, N., and Hattie, J. (1996)
Cultural differences in the use of strategies for self-regulated learning. *American Journal of Educational Research, 33,* 845-871.

Purdie, N., Hattie, J., and Douglas, G. (1996)
Students' conceptions of learning and their use of self-regulated learning strategies: A cross-cultural comparison. *Journal of Educational Psychology, 88,* 87-100.

93

Quinn, M.M., Kavale, K.A., Mathur, S.R., Rutherford, R.B., and Forness, S.R. (1999)
A meta-analysis of social skill interventions for students with emotional or behavioral disorders. *Journal of Emotional and Behavioral Disorders, 7*(1), 54-64.

Rabinowitz, M., and McAuley, R. (1990)
Conceptual knowledge processing: An oxymoron? In W. Schneider and F.E. Weinert (Eds.), *Interactions among aptitudes, strategies, and knowledge in cognitive performance* (pp. 117-133). New York: Springer-Verlag.

Rausch, M.K., and Skiba, R.J. (2004)
Unplanned outcomes: Suspensions and expulsions in Indiana. Bloomington, IN: Center for Evaluation and Education Policy.

Resnick, M.D., et al. (1997)
Protecting adolescents from harm: Findings from the National Longitudinal Study on Adolescent Health, *Journal of the American Medical Association, 278*(10), 823-832.

Reyes, O., Gillock, K., and Kobus, K. (1994)
A longitudinal study of school adjustment in urban, minority adolescents: Effects of a high school transition program. *American Journal of Community Psychology, 22,* 341-369.

Reynolds, R.E., Wade, S.E., Trathen, W., and Lapan, R. (1989)
The selective attention strategy and prose learning. In M. Pressley, C. McCormick, and E. Miller (Eds.), *Cognitive strategies research* (pp. 159-190). New York: Springer-Verlag.

Robbins, S.B., Lauver, K., Le, H., Davis, D., Langley, R., and Carlstrom, A. (2004)
Do psychosocial and study skill factors predict college outcomes? A meta-analysis. *Psychological Bulletin, 130*(2), 261-288.

Roberts, B.W., and Del Vecchio, W.F. (2000)
The rank-order consistency of personality traits from childhood to old age: A quantitative review of longitudinal studies. *Psychological Bulletin, 126,* 3-25.

Robinson, G.E., and Craver, J.M. (1989)
Assessing and grading student achievement. Arlington, VA: Educational Research Service.

Roderick, M. (1991)
The path to dropping out among public school youth: Middle school and early high school experiences. Dissertation Series # D-91-2. Cambridge, MA. Malcolm Weiner Center for Social Policy, John F. Kennedy School of Government, Harvard University.

Roderick, M. (1993)
The path to dropping out: Evidence for intervention. Westport, CT: Auburn House, Greenwood Publishing Group.

Roderick, M. (1994)
Grade retention and school dropout: Investigating the association. *American Educational Research Journal, 31*(4), 729-759.

Roderick, M., and Camburn, E. (1996)
Academic difficulty during the high school transition. In P.B. Sebring, A.S. Bryk, M. Roderick, and E. Camburn (Eds.), *Charting reform in Chicago: The students speak.* Chicago: University of Chicago Consortium on Chicago School Research.

Roderick, M., and Camburn, E. (1999)
Risk and recovery from course failure in the early years of high school. *American Educational Research Journal, 36*(2), 303-343.

Roderick, M., and Nagaoka, J. (2008)
Increasing college access and graduation among Chicago public high school graduates. In McPherson, M.S. and Shapiro, M.O. (Eds.) *College success what it means and how to make it happen* (pp. 19-66). New York: College Board Publications.

Roderick M., Nagaoka, J., and Allensworth, E. (2006)
From high school to the future: A first look at Chicago public school graduates' college enrollment, college preparation, and graduation from four-year colleges. Chicago: University of Chicago Consortium on Chicago School Research.

Roderick, M., Nagaoka, J., and Coca, V. (2009)
College readiness for all: The challenge for urban high schools. *The Future of Children, 19*(1), 185-210.

Roderick, M., Nagaoka, J., Coca, V., and Moeller, E. (2008)
From high school to the future: Potholes on the road to college. Chicago: University of Chicago Consortium on Chicago School Research.

Rosen, J.A. (2010)
Academic self-concept. In J.A. Rosen, E.J. Glennie, B.W. Dalton, J.M. Lennon, and R.N. Bozick (Eds.), *Noncognitive skills in the classroom: New perspectives on educational research* (pp. 117-144). Research Triangle Park, NC: RTI International.

Rosen, J.A., Glennie, E.J., Dalton, B.W., Lennon, J.M., and Bozick, R.N. (2010)
Noncognitive skills in the classroom: New perspectives on educational research. Research Triangle Park, NC: RTI International.

Rosenkranz, T., de la Torre, M., Allensworth, E., and Stevens, W.D. (Forthcoming)
Free to Fail Research Series: Grades drop when students enter high school. Chicago: University of Chicago Consortium on Chicago School Research.

Rosenthal, R., and Jacobson, L. (1968)
Pygmalion in the classroom. New York: Holt, Rinehart, and Winston.

Roseth, C.J., Johnson, D.W., and Johnson, R.T. (2008)
Promoting early adolescents' achievement and peer relationships: The effects of cooperative, competitive, and individualistic goal structures. *Psychological Bulletin, 134*(2), 223-246.

94

Rotter, J.B. (1954)
Social learning and clinical psychology. NY: Prentice-Hall.

Ryan, J.F. (2004)
The relationship between institutional expenditures and degree attainment at baccalaureate college. *Research in Higher Education, 45*(2), 97-114.

Ryan, R.M., and Deci, E.L. (2000)
Self-determination theory and the facilitation of intrinsic motivation, social development, and well-being. *American Psychologist, 55*, 68-78.

Sarafino, E.P. (2001)
Behavior Modification (2nd ed.). Boston: McGraw-Hill.

Schaps, E., Battistich, V., and Solomon, D. (2004)
Community in school as key to student growth: Findings from the Child Development Project. In J.E. Zins, R.P. Weissberg, M.C. Wang, and H.J. Walberg (Eds.), *Building academic success on social and emotional learning: What does the research say?* (pp. 189-205). New York: Teachers College Press.

Schmeck, R.R. (1988)
Individual differences and learning strategies. In C.E. Weinstein, E.T. Goetz, and P.A. Alexander (Eds.). *Learning and study strategies: Issues in assessment, instruction, and evaluation* (pp. 171-191). San Diego, CA: Academic Press.

Schmidt, F.L., and Hunter, J.E. (1998)
The validity and utility of selection methods in personnel psychology: Practical and theoretical implications of 85 years of research findings. *Psychological Bulletin, 124*(2), 262-274.

Schmitt, N., Billington, A., Keeney, J., Reeder, M., Pleskac, T., Sinha, R., and Zorzie, M. (2011)
Development and validation of measures of noncognitive college student potential. Retrieved from http://professionals.collegeboard.com/profdownload/pdf/10b_1555_Dvlpmnt_and_Validation_WEB_110315.pdf.

Schoenfeld, A.H. (1985)
Mathematical problem solving. Orlando, FL: Academic Press.

Schoenfeld, A.H. (1987)
Cognitive science and mathematics education: An overview. In A.H. Schoenfeld (Ed.), *Cognitive science and mathematics education* (pp. 1-31). Hillsdale, NJ: Erlbaum.

Schulenberg, J.E., Asp, C.E., and Petersen, A.C. (1984)
School for the young adolescent's perspective: A descriptive report. *Journal of Early Adolescence, 4*, 107-130.

Schunk, D.H., and Hanson, A.R. (1985)
Peer models: Influence on children's self-efficacy and achievement. *Journal of Educational Psychology, 77*, 313-322.

Scott, M., Bailey, T., and Kienzl, G. (2006)
Relative success? Determinants of college graduation rates in public and private colleges in the U.S. *Research in Higher Education, 47*(3), 249-279.

Seidman, E., LaRue, A., Aber, L.J., Mitchell, C., and Feinman, J. (1994)
The impact of school transitions in early adolescence on the self-system and perceived social context of poor urban youth. *Child Development, 65*, 507-522.

Seligman, M., and Maier, S. (1967)
Failure to escape traumatic shock. *Journal of Experimental Psychology, 74*, 1-9.

Sherman, D.K., Cohen, G.L., Nelson, L.D., Nussbaum, A.D., Bunyan, D.P., and Garcia, J.P. (2009)
Affirmed yet unaware: Exploring the role of awareness in the process of self-affirmation. *Journal of Personality and Social Psychology, 97*, 745-764.

Shoda, Y., Mischel, W., and Peake, P.K. (1990)
Predicting adolescent cognitive and self-regulatory competencies from preschool delay of gratification: Identifying diagnostic conditions. *Developmental Psychology, 26*(6), 978-986.

Shouse, R.C. (1996)
Academic press and sense of community: Conflict, congruence, and implications for student achievement. *Social Psychology of Education, 1*(1), 47-68.

Simmons, R.G., Black, A., and Zhou, Y. (1991)
African American versus White children and the transition into junior high school. *American Journal of Education, 99*, 481-520.

Simmons, R.G., and Blyth, D.A. (1987)
Moving into adolescence: The impact of pubertal change and school context. Hawthorn, NY: Aldine de Gruyter.

Simmons-Morton, B.G., Crump, A.D., Haynie, D.L., and Saylor, K.E. (1999)
Student-school bonding and adolescent problem behavior. *Health Education Research, 14*(1), 99-107.

Sinclair, M.F., Christenson, S.L., Evelo, D.L., and Hurley, C.M. (1998)
Dropout prevention for youth with disabilities: Efficacy of a sustained school engagement procedure. *Exceptional Children, 65*(1), 7-21.

Skiba, R.J., Simmons, A.B., Ritter, S., Gibb, A.C., Rausch, M.K., and Cuadrado, J. (2008)
Achieving equity in special education: History, status, and current challenges. *Exceptional Children, 74*, 264-288.

Skiba, R.J., Michael, R.S., Nardo, A.C., and Peterson, R.L. (2002)
The color of discipline: Sources of racial and gender disproportionality in school punishment. *Urban Review, 34*, 317-342.

Skinner, B.F. (1953)
Science and human behavior. New York: Free Press.

Slavin, R.E. (1995)
Cooperative learning (2nd ed.). Needham Heights, MA: Allyn and Bacon.

Snow, R.E., Corno, L., and Jackson, D. (1996)
Individual differences in affective and conative functions.
In D. Berliner and R. Calfee, Eds., *Handbook of educational psychology* (pp. 243-310). New York: Macmillan.

Snow, R.E., and Swanson, J. (1992)
Instructional psychology: Aptitude, adaptation, and assessment. *Annual Review of Psychology, 43*, 583-626.

Solomon, D., Watson, M., Battistich, V., Schaps, E., and Delucchi, K. (1996)
Creating classrooms that students experience as communities. *American Journal of Community Psychology, 24*(6), 719-748.

Somers, P. (1995)
A comprehensive model for examining the impact of financial aid on enrollment and persistence. *Journal of Student Financial Aid, 25*(1), 13-27.

Somers, P. (1996)
The influence of price on year-to-year persistence of college students. *NASPA Journal, 33*(2), 94-103.

Srivastava, S., John, O.P., Gosling, S.D., and Potter, J. (2003)
Development of personality in early and middle adulthood: Set like plaster or persistent change? *Journal of Personality and Social Psychology, 84*(5), 1041–1053.

Staats, A.W. (1963)
Complex human behavior. New York: Holt, Rinehart and Winston.

Steele, C.M. (1992)
Race and the schooling of Black Americans. *The Atlantic Monthly, 269*(4), 68-78.

Steele, C.M. (1997)
A threat in the air: How stereotypes shape intellectual identity and performance. *American Psychologist, 52*, 613-629.

Steele, C.M., and Aronson, J. (1995)
Stereotype threat and the intellectual test performance of African Americans. *Journal of Personality and Social Psychology, 69*(5), 797-811.

Stefanou, C.R., Perencevich, K.C., DiCintio, M., and Turner, J.C. (2004)
Supporting autonomy in the classroom: Ways teachers encourage student decision making and ownership. *Educational Psychologist, 39*(4), 97-110.

Stevens, W.D., Allensworth, E., de la Torre, M., Rosenkranz, T., Pareja, A.S., Johnson, D.W., Patton, D., and Brown, E. (Forthcoming)
Free to Fail Research Series: Why effort drops and how it leads to low grades. Chicago: University of Chicago Consortium on Chicago School Research.

Stewart, E.A., Schreck, C.J., and Simons, R.L. (2006)
"I ain't gonna let no one disrespect me": Does the code of the street reduce or increase violent victimization among African American adolescents? *Journal of Research in Crime and Delinquency, 43*, 427-458.

Stiggins, R.J. (1997)
Student-centered classroom assessment (2nd ed.). Columbus, OH: Merrill.

Stiggins, R.J., Frisbie, D.A., and Griswold, P.A. (1989)
Inside high school grading practices: Building a research agenda. *Educational Measurement: Issues and Practices, 8*(2), 5-14.

Stipek, D.J. (1986)
Children's motivation to learn. In T.M. Tomlinson and H J. Walberg (Eds.), *Academic work and educational excellence* (pp. 197-221). Berkeley, CA: McCutchan.

Stipek, D.J. (2001)
Motivation to learn: Integrating theory and practice (4th ed.). Boston: Allyn and Bacon.

St. John, E., Andrieu, S., Oescher, J., and Starkey, J.B. (1994)
The Influence of Student Aid on Within-Year Persistence by Traditional College-Age Students in Four-Year Colleges. *Research in Higher Education, 35*(4), pp. 455-480.

Sweller, J. (1988)
Cognitive load during problem solving: effects on learning. *Cognitive Science, 12*, 257-285.

Tangney, J.P., Baumeister, R.F., and Boone, A.L. (2004)
High self-control predicts good adjustment, less pathology, better grades, and interpersonal success. *Journal of Personality, 72*, 271-322.

Terenzini, P.T., Springer, L., Yaeger, P.M., Pascarella, E.T., and Nora, A. (1996)
First-generation college students: Characteristics, experiences, and cognitive development. *Research in Higher Education, 37*(1), 1-22.

Teo, A., Carlson, E., Mathieu, P.J., Egeland, B., and Sroufe, L.A. (1996)
A prospective longitudinal study of psychosocial predictors of achievement. *Journal of School Psychology, 34*, 285-306.

Thomas, S.L. (2000)
Ties that bind: A social network approach to understanding student integration and persistence. *The Journal of Higher Education, 71*(5), 591-615.

Tierney, W.G. (1999)
Models of minority college-going and retention: Cultural integrity versus cultural suicide. *Journal of Negro Education, 68*(1), 80-91.

Tinto, V. (1987)
Leaving college: Rethinking the causes and cures of student attrition. Chicago: University of Chicago Press.

Tinto, V., and Goodsell-Love, A. (1993)
Building community. *Liberal Education, 79*(4), 16.

Titus, M. (2004)
An examination of the influence of institutional context on student persistence at four-year colleges and universities: A multilevel approach. *Research in Higher Education, 45*(7), 673-699.

Titus, M. (2006a)
Understanding college degree completion of students with low socioeconomic status: The influence of the institutional financial context. *Research in Higher Education, 47*(4), 371-398.

Titus, M. (2006b)
Understanding the influence of the financial context of institutions on student persistence at four-year colleges and universities. *Journal of Higher Education, 77*(2), 353-375.

Tough, P. (2011, Sept 14)
What if the secret to success is failure? *The New York Times Magazine.* Retrieved from http://www.nytimes. com/ 2011/09/18/magazine/what-if-the-secret-to-success-is-failure.html?_r=1&pagewanted=all.

Trilling, B., and Fadel, C. (2009)
Twenty-first century skills: Learning for life in our times. San Francisco: Jossey-Bass.

Tross, S.A., Harper, J.P., Osher, L.W., and Kneidinger, L.M. (2000)
Not just the usual cast of characteristics: Using personality to predict college student performance and retention. *Journal of College Student Development, 41*(3), 323-334.

Tyler R.W. (1949)
Basic prnciples of curriculum and instruction. Chicago: University of Chicago Press.

Tyler, R.W. (2000)
A rationale for program evaluation. In D.L. Stufflebeam, G.F. Madaus, and T. Kelleghan (Eds.), *Evaluation models: Viewpoints on educational and human service evaluation* (2nd ed.). (pp. 87-96). Boston: Kluwer Academic Publishers.

van de Weil, N., Matthys, W., Cohen-Kettenis, P.C., and van Engeland, H. (2002)
Effective treatments of school-aged conduct disordered children: Recommendations for changing clinical and research practices. *European Child & Adolescent Psychiatry, 11,* 79-84.

Van Lehn, K. (1996)
Cognitive skill acquisition. *Annual Review of Psychology, 47,* 513-539.

Van Ryzin, M. (2010)
Secondary school advisors as mentors and secondary attachment figures. *Journal of Community Psychology, 38,* 131-154.

Vavrus, F., and Cole, K.M. (2002)
"I didn't do nothin'": The discursive construction of school suspension. *Urban Review, 34,* 87-111.

Vispoel, W.P., and Austin, J.R. (1995)
Success and failure in junior high school: A critical incident approach to understanding students' attributional beliefs. *American Educational Research Journal, 32*(2), 377-412.

Vygotsky, L.S. (1978)
Mind in society: The development of higher psychological processes. Cambridge, MA: Harvard University Press.

Wallace, J.M., Goodkind, S., Wallace, C.M., and Bachman, J.G. (2008)
Racial, ethnic, and gender differences in school discipline among U.S. high school students: 1991-2005. *Negro Educational Review, 59,* 47-62.

Walton, G.M., and Cohen, G.L. (2007)
A question of belonging: Race, social fit, and achievement. *Journal of Personality and Social Psychology, 92,* 82-96.

Walton, G.M., and Cohen, G.L. (2011)
A brief social-belonging intervention improves academic and health outcomes among minority students. *Science, 331,* 1447-1451.

Walton, G.M., and Dweck, C.S. (2009)
Solving social problems like a psychologist. *Perspectives on Psychological Science, 4,* 101-102.

Walton, G.M., and Spencer, S.J. (2009)
Latent ability: Grades and test scores systematically underestimate the intellectual ability of negatively stereotyped students. *Psychological Science, 20,* 1132-1139.

Wang, M.C., Haertel, G.D., and Walberg, H.J. (1994)
What helps students learn? *Educational Leadership, 51,* 74-79.

Ward, W.E., Banks, W.C., and Wilson, S. (1991)
Delayed gratification in Blacks. In R.L. Jones (Ed.), *Black psychology* (3rd ed.) (pp. 167-180). Berkeley, CA: Cobb and Henry.

Weick, K.E. (1995)
Sensemaking in organizations. Thousand Oaks, CA: Sage Publications.

Weiner, B. (1979)
A theory of motivation for some classroom experiences. *Journal of Educational Psychology, 71*(1), 3-25.

Weiner, B. (1986)
An attributional theory of emotion and motivation. New York: Springer-Verlag.

97

Weinstein, C.E., and Mayer, R.E. (1986)
The teaching of learning strategies. In M. Wittrock,
Handbook of research on teaching (pp. 315-327).
New York: Macmillan.

Weinstein, C.E., Schulte, A., and Palmer, D.R. (1987)
The learning and study strategies inventory. Clearwater, FL:
H & H Publishing.

Weissberg, R.P., Caplan, M.Z., and Sivo, P.J. (1989)
A new conceptual framework for establishing school-
based social competence promotion programs. In
L.A. Bond and B.E. Compas (Eds.), *Primary prevention
and promotion in the schools* (pp. 255-296). Newbury Park,
CA: Sage.

Wentzel, K.R. (1991)
Social competence at school: Relations between
social responsibility and academic achievement.
Review of Educational Research, 61, 1-24.

Wentzel, K.R. (1993)
Does being good make the grade? Social behavior and
academic competence in middle school. *Journal of
Educational Psychology, 85,* 357-364.

Wentzel, K.R. (1994)
Relations of social goal pursuit to social acceptance, and
perceived social support. *Journal of Education Psychology,
86,* 173-182.

Wentzel, K.R. (2002)
Are effective teachers like good parents? Interpersonal
predictors of school adjustment in early adolescence.
Child Development, 73, 287-301.

Wentzel, K.B., and Asher, S.R. (1995)
The academic lives of neglected, rejected, popular, and
controversial children. *Child Development, 66,* 754-763.

Wentzel, K.R., and Caldwell, K. (1997)
Friendships, peer acceptance, and group membership:
Relations to academic achievement in middle school.
Child Development, 68(6), 1198-1209.

Whelage, G.G., and Rutter, R.A. (1986)
Dropping out: How much do schools contribute to the
problem? *Teachers College Record, 87,* 372-393.

White, B.Y., and Fredericksen, J.R. (1994, Fall)
Using assessment to foster a classroom research
community. *Educator,* 19-24.

White, B.Y., and Frederiksen, J.R. (1998)
Inquiry, modeling, and metacognition: Making science
accessible to all students. *Cognition and Instruction, 16* (1),
3-118.

Wigfield, A. (1994)
Expectancy-value theory of achievement motivation:
A developmental perspective. *Educational Psychology
Review, 6,* 49-78.

Wigfield, A., and Eccles, J.S. (1992)
The development of achievement task values: A theoretical
analysis. *Developmental Review, 12,* 265-310.

Wigfield, A., and Eccles, J.S. (2000)
Expectancy-value theory of achievement motivation.
Contemporary Educational Psychology, 25, 68-81.

Wilson, T.D. (2006)
The power of social psychological interventions.
Science, 313, 1251-1252.

Wilson, T.D., and Linville, P.W. (1982)
Improving the academic performance of college freshmen:
Attribution therapy revisited. *Journal of Personality and
Social Psychology, 42,* 367-376.

Wilson, T.D., and Linville, P.W. (1985)
Improving the performance of college freshmen with
attributional techniques. *Journal of Personality and
Social Psychology, 49,* 287-293.

Winne, P.H. (1979)
Experiments relating teachers' use of higher cognitive
questions to student achievement. *Review of Educational
Research, 49*(1), 13-50.

Winne, P.H. (1985)
Steps toward promoting cognitive achievements.
Elementary School Journal, 85, 673-693.

Winne, P.H. (1996)
A metacogntive view of individual differences in
self-regulated learning. *Learning and Individual
Differences, 8*(4), 327-353.

Winne, P.H. (1997)
Experimenting to bootstrap self-regulated learning.
Journal of Educational Psychology, 89(3), 397-410.

Winne, P.H., and Hadwin, A.F. (1998)
Studying as self-regulated learning. In D.J. Hacker,
J. Dunlosky, and A.C. Graesser (Eds.), *Metacognition in
educational theory and practice* (pp. 277-304). Hillsdale,
NJ: Erlbaum.

Winne, P.H., Jamieson-Noel, D., and Muis, K.R. (2002)
Methodological issues and advances in researching
tactics, strategies, and self-regulated learning. In
P.R. Pintrich and M.L. Maehr (Eds.), *New directions
in measures and methods.* Vol. 12 (pp. 121-155).
Greenwich, CT: JAI Press.

Winne, P.H., and Nesbit, J. (2010)
The psychology of academic achievement.
Annual Review of Psychology, 61, 653-678.

Winne, P.H., Nesbit, J.C., Kumar, V., Hadwin, A.F.,
Lajoie, S.P., Azevedo, R., and Perry, N. (2006)
Supporting self-regulated learning with gStudy
software: The learning kit project. *Technology,
Instruction, Cognition, and Learning, 3,* 105-113.

Wolfe, M.L. (1981)
Forecasting summative evaluation from formative evaluation: A double cross-validation study. *Psychological Reports, 49*, 843-848.

Wolfe, R.N., and Johnson, S.D. (1995)
Personality as a predictor of college performance. *Educational and Psychological Measurement, 55*, 177-185.

Wood, E., Woloshyn, V.E., and Willoughby, T. (Eds.). (1995)
Cognitive strategy instruction for middle and high schools. Cambridge, MA: Brookline Books.

Yair, G. (2000)
Educational battlefields in America: The tug-of-war over students' engagement with instruction. *Sociology of Education, 73*, 247-269.

Yeager, D., Muhich, J., Asera, R., and Torres, L. (2011, Jan 30)
90-day cycle report: Productive persistence. Presentation at the STATWAY Winter Institute. Carnegie Foundation for the Advancement of Teaching, Palo Alto, California. PowerPoint presentation retrieved January 21, 2012, from http://207.62.63.167/departments/mathematics/statway_talk.pdf.

Yeager, D.S., and Walton, G.M. (2011)
Social-psychological interventions in education: They're not magic. *Review of Educational Research, 81*(2), 267-301.

Yurgelun-Todd, D. (2007)
Emotional and cognitive changes during adolescence. *Current Opinion in Neurobiology, 17*, 251-257.

Zau, A.C., and Betts, J.R. (2008)
Predicting success, preventing failure: An investigation of the California High School Exit Exam. Report of the Public Policy Institute of California.

Zheng, J.L., Saunders, K.P., Shelley II, M.C., and Whalen, D.F. (2002)
Predictors of academic success for freshmen residence hall students. *Journal of College Student Development, 43*(2), 267-283.

Zimmerman, B.J. (1990)
Self-regulated learning and academic achievement: An overview. *Educational Psychologist, 25*(1), 3-17.

Zimmerman, B.J. (2001)
Self-regulated learning. In N.J. Smelser and P.B. Baltes (Eds.). *International Encyclopedia of the Social and Behavioral Sciences* (pp. 13855-13859). New York: Elsevier Ltd.

Zimmerman, B.J., and Martinez-Pons, M. (1986)
Development of a structured interview for assessing student use of self-regulated learning strategies. *American Educational Research Journal, 23*, 614-628.

Zimmerman, B.J., and Pons, M. (1988)
Construct validation of a strategy model of student self-regulated learning. *Journal of Educational Psychology, 80*, 284-290.

Zimmerman, B.J., and Schunk, D.H. (Eds.). (1989)
Self-regulated learning and academic achievement: Theory, research, and practice. New York: Springer Verlag.

Endnotes

Chapter 1

1   This is not to suggest that the academic content of a course does not matter. Challenging academic work is an essential ingredient in preparing students for college. However, mere exposure to rigorous content does not increase learning. Students' performance in their classes—how well they are doing the work that is assigned to them—is a much better indicator of their future success than is the course title or their test scores.

2   A one standard deviation increase in high school GPA was associated with a 0.34 standard deviation increase in college GPA. The SAT II writing test, the SAT component that has the strongest association with grades in college, was correlated with only a 0.19 standard deviation increase in college GPA.

Chapter 3

3   Both studying time and senior grades were self-reported, which may account for the relatively high average course grades reported. The authors suggest that truncated measures from self-reports are likely to attenuate the size of the effects. In other words, if study time were measured directly and course grades were taken from transcripts, the effect of homework time on grades would likely be larger.

Chapter 6

4   Self-regulated learning is a very specific form of self-regulation, and should be considered as distinct from behavioral self-regulation more broadly, which is largely about impulse control. Self-regulated learning shares with self-regulation a focus on the ability to make conscious choices to direct the self and the ability to alter one's responses or one's behavior to align or conform to particular ideals, standards, norms, rules, agreements, or plans. However, self-regulated learning deals primarily with mental processes and metacognition rather than behavioral control.

5   Winne and Hadwin (1998) note that the learner's goals are not necessarily aligned with the teacher's goals. The teacher might assign a task that involves reading a chapter from a physics textbook and then completing a set of questions, while a student's goal might be to find someone from whom he can copy the homework and thus avoid reading the chapter.

6   This becomes a challenge in measuring students' use of learning strategies when those measures rely on student self-report of strategy use.

7   Sample items include: "I ask myself questions to make sure I know the material I have been studying," "I find that when the teacher is talking I think of other things and don't really listen to what is being said," and "I often find that I have been reading for class but don't know what it is all about. "

Chapter 7

8   Note that in this review we do not examine the broader work on social-emotional learning. An adolescent's demonstration of social skills can be understood as the physical manifestation of underlying social-emotional factors such as emotional awareness or emotional "intelligence" and emotional self-regulation. This is an area worthy of further study which could well contribute to a deeper understanding of the role of noncognitive factors in school performance.

9   Suspension is defined as "temporarily removed from regular school activities either in or out of school...due to a behavior problem."

Chapter 8: Case Study 2

10   The Ninth Grade Success Academy is part of the Talent Development High School model. The Success Academy is designed to increase structure and support for freshmen by combining three approaches: 1) keeping groups of ninth-graders together who share the same classes and same teachers in a school-within-a-school model; 2) using blocked scheduling to reduce the number of classes freshmen take and providing specialized courses for ninth-graders to transition them to high-school-level work, and 3) providing professional development supports and structures for teachers to work together (Kemple, Herlihy, & Smith, 2005).

11   A student is considered on-track if he or she has accumulated five full credits (10 semester credits) and has no more than one semester F in a core subject (English, math, science, or social science) by the end of the first year in high school. This is an indicator of the minimal expected level of performance. Students in CPS need 24 credits to graduate from high school, so a student with only five credits at the end of freshman year will need to pass courses at a faster rate in later years (Miller, Allensworth, & Kochanek, 2002).

12 Allensworth & Easton (2007) estimate that, even after controlling for the demographic characteristics and entering test scores of freshmen, the predicted probability of graduation was 55 percentage points higher (81 versus 26 percent) for a student who was on- versus off-track at the end of freshman year.

Appendix

Educational Attainment by Gender, Race/Ethnicity is Driven by Differences in GPA

There are large and persistent gaps in educational attainment by students' race, ethnicity, and gender. Asian American and White students graduate from high school and attend college at much higher rates than African American and Latino students. Girls graduate from high school and attend college at higher rates than boys. Much of the conversation around college readiness focuses on students' college entrance exams—scores on the ACT and the SAT. However, it is not low test scores that explain gaps in educational attainment. What really drives the differences in educational attainment by gender and race/ethnicity are differences in students' course grades, or GPA.

While African American and Latino CPS students have lower average ACT scores than White and Asian American CPS students, it is actually course failures and low GPAs that create significant barriers to high school graduation, college access, and college graduation for African American and Latino students. Differences in course grades by race and ethnicity explain most of the gaps in educational attainment (Allensworth & Easton, 2007; Roderick, Nagaoka, & Allensworth,

2006). Differences in high school GPA also explain all of the gender gap in college attendance and college graduation among Chicago high school graduates. Boys do not have lower ACT scores than girls, on average, but their grades are considerably lower; almost half of boys (47 percent) graduate with less than a C average, compared to about a quarter of girls (27 percent) (Roderick, Nagaoka, & Allensworth, 2006). These patterns are mirrored in national data. Using a nationally representative sample, Jacob (2002) found that students' course grades explained a large proportion of the gender gap in college enrollment. Despite similar test score performance, males were less likely to attend college because of lower grades.

In order to address racial, ethnic, and gender differences in educational attainment, it becomes crucial to focus on the GPA gaps as an important lever to explain high school graduation and college enrollment. Yet, the 2009 National Assessment of Educational Progress (NAEP) transcript study shows that from 1990 to 2009 gaps in GPAs by race/ethnicity and gender were persistent and showed no sign of improving (see Figures A.1 and A.2).

Figure A.1
National Trend in Average GPAs by Race/Ethnicity: 1990-2009

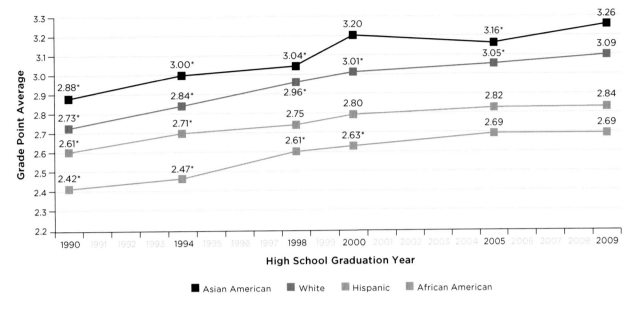

SOURCE: U.S. Department of Education, Institute of Education Sciences,
National Center for Education Statistics, High School Transcript Study (HSTS),
various years, 1990-2009.

* Significantly different (p<.05) from 2009.

Figure A.2
National Trend in Average GPAs by Gender: 1990-2009

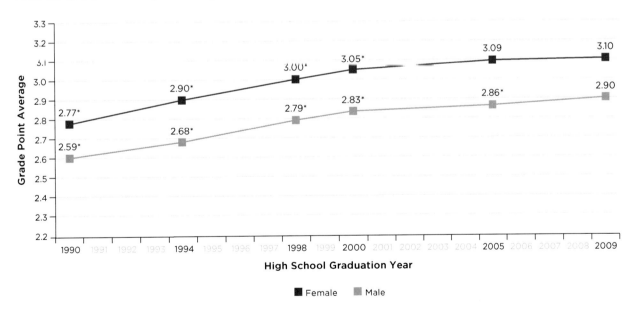

SOURCE: U.S. Department of Education, Institute of Education Sciences,
National Center for Education Statistics, High School Transcript Study (HSTS),
various years, 1990-2009.

* Significantly different (p<.05) from 2009.

Appendix

ABOUT THE AUTHORS

CAMILLE A. FARRINGTON, PHD, is a Research Associate (Assistant Professor) at the School of Social Service Administration (SSA) at the University of Chicago and a research affiliate at CCSR. She serves as Director of Curriculum, Instruction, and Assessment at the Network for College Success at SSA, working with Chicago Public Schools (CPS) transformation high schools as part of a federal School Improvement Grant. Her research interests focus on policy and practice in urban high school reform, particularly classroom instruction and assessment, academic rigor, tracking, and dropout. She is author of a forthcoming book on school structures and practices that perpetuate student failure (winter 2012, Teachers College Press). She worked for 15 years as a public high school educator and administrator. Dr. Farrington received a BA from the University of California at Santa Cruz and a PhD in Policy Studies in Urban Education from the University of Illinois at Chicago.

MELISSA RODERICK, PHD, is the Hermon Dunlap Smith Professor at SSA and a senior director at CCSR where she leads the organization's postsecondary research. Professor Roderick is also the co-director of the Network for College Success, a network of high schools focused on developing high-quality leadership and student performance in Chicago's high schools. Professor Roderick is an expert in urban school reform, high school reform, high-stakes testing, minority adolescent development, and school transitions. Her new work focuses on understanding the relationship between students' high school careers and preparation, their college selection choices and their postsecondary outcomes through linked quantitative and qualitative research. From 2001 to 2003, Professor Roderick served as Director of Planning and Development for CPS. Professor Roderick has a PhD from the Committee on Public Policy from Harvard University, a master's degree in Public Policy from the John F. Kennedy School of Government at Harvard University, and an AB from Bowdoin College.

ELAINE ALLENSWORTH, PHD, is the Interim Executive Director of CCSR. She conducts research on factors affecting school improvement and students' educational attainment, including high school graduation, college readiness, curriculum and instruction, and school organization and leadership. Her work on early indicators of high school graduation has been adopted for tracking systems used in Chicago and other districts across the country. Dr. Allensworth is one of the authors of the book, *Organizing Schools for Improvement: Lessons from Chicago*, which provides a detailed analysis of school practices and community conditions that promote school improvement. One of her current projects examines the ways in which students' achievement in the middle grades interacts with their experiences in high school to affect postsecondary success, funded by the Bill & Melinda Gates Foundation. Dr. Allensworth holds a PhD in Sociology from Michigan State University. She was once a high school Spanish and science teacher.

JENNY NAGAOKA is the Deputy Director of CCSR. Her current work uses linked quantitative and qualitative methods to examine the relationship among high school preparation, college choice, and postsecondary outcomes for CPS students. Her research interests focus on urban education reform, particularly developing school environments and instructional practices that promote college readiness and success. Her previous work includes research on quality of classroom instruction, Chicago's retention policy, and an evaluation of the effects of a summer school program.

TASHA SENECA KEYES is a second-year doctoral student at SSA. She worked as a school social worker in Utah before returning to school. She received her MSW from the University of Utah and her BA from Brigham Young University. She is currently working with the Chicago Post-secondary Transition Project at CCSR, to understand college choice and college match. Her research interests include how school context matters for adolescent identity and self-concept development, particularly for mixed race and Native American youth, and creating supportive school settings to increase sense of belonging and engagement for minority students and families.

DAVID W. JOHNSON is a research assistant at the Chicago Postsecondary Transition Project at CCSR and a doctoral candidate at SSA. His dissertation research focuses on how high school culture and climate affect students' college search, application, and college choices. His research interests broadly include school culture and climate, adolescent development, and postsecondary access and attainment among low income, minority, and first-generation college students.

NICOLE O. BEECHUM is a third-year doctoral student at SSA. She received her AM from SSA in 2006 and a BA in Political Science from Mount Saint Mary's College in Los Angeles in 2001. She is currently working on various projects for the Chicago Postsecondary Transition Project at CCSR, including research examining the International Baccalaureate (IB) program at CPS and understanding college match among CPS graduates. Her research interests include the school-level factors that affect academic identities and academic outcomes for African American adolescent males in large urban school districts.

This report reflects the interpretation of the authors. Although CCSR's Steering Committee provided technical advice, no formal endorsement by these individuals, organizations, or the full Consortium should be assumed.